AF655243

Teaching Yourself Spanish

Teaching Yourself
SPANISH

RAMESH KUMAR

MAHAVEER PUBLISHERS

Published by
MAHAVEER PUBLISHERS
4764/2A, 23-Ansari Road, Daryaganj
New Delhi - 110002
Ph. : 011 – 66629669–79–89
Fax : 011 – 41563419
e-mail : mahaveerpublishers@gmail.com

© Mahaveer Publishers

All rights reserved. No part of this publication may be reproduced, stored in a retrieval system, or transmitted, in any form or by any means, electronic, mechanical, photocopying, recording or otherwise, without the prior written permission of the publishers.

First Edition : 2005
Revised Edition : 2011

Teaching Yourself Spanish
ISBN : 9788190219686

Distributed by
VAIBHAV BOOK SERVICE
e-mail : vaibhavbookservice@gmail.com

Published by D.K. Jha for Mahaveer Publishers
Printed by Jaico Printers, New Delhi

PREFACE

Spanish is a language which has got its origin from 'Latin'. Sounds and phonetics are soft and sharp, so it is also called a 'Romantic Language'. Spanish is spoken in a vast area, hence the demand for professionals equipped with spoken and written Spanish is also much more than any other language. It is the principal language of countries besides Spain. Spanish is also the main language in Peru, Uruguay, Cuba, Chile, Paraguay, Philippines, Panama, America, etc. It is the second most important language in some other countries.

We have put in our best effort to present the language in a simple and comprehensible way so that even the beginner can have a basic knowledge of Spanish. Still we will appreciate any suggestion from our readers and well-wishers.

CONTENTS

The Alphabets & Pronunciation

Spanish is basically an easy language to pronounce because almost all its sounds are similar to the ones found in SPANISH, or in other Indian language having their origin in the Sanskrit language. Each sound is pronounced in the same way every time it occurs and the written form of words is very close to the spoken form. Once you have mastered the five main vowels (the equivalent of which is also given in SPANISH) and the consonants, it becomes easy to read and write Spanish.

The Spanish Vowels

a (आ) pronounced as 'a' in 'father'

dar	*casa*	*mesa*
दार	कासा	मेसा

e (ए) pronounced as 'e' in 'elephant'

clase	*necesario*	*leer*	*eso*
क्लासे	नेसेसारिओ	लेएर	एसो

i (ई) pronounced as 'ee' in 'seen'

ir	*decir*	*venir*	*sentir*
ईर	देसीर	वेनीर	सेन्तीर

o (ओ) pronounced as 'o' in 'four'

	otro	*todo*	*eso*	*señor*
	ओत्रो	तोदो	एसो	सेन्योर
u (ऊ)	pronounced as 'oo' in 'root'			
	mucho	*pluma*	*buscar*	*estudiar*
	मूचो	प्लूमा	बुस्कार	एस्तूदियार

The Spanish Consonants

b/v (बे) Both the consonants are very similar to the English 'b'

beber	*bastante*	*butano*
बेबेर	बास्तान्ते	बुतानो

c (i) (से) Used before 'i' and 'e' is pronounced as 'th' as in 'thin', mainly in Spain. The point of sound articulation is dental-fricative. As phoneme it is not available in the SPANISH language although the closet will be an aspirated थ ।

In Latin American Spanish it sounds like 'c' in 'ice'. For sheer convenience we shall mostly use this variety hence forward.

nación	*decir*	*ciencia*
नासीयोन	देसीर	सीएन्सिया

(ii) (क) Used before 'a', 'o' and 'u', or a consonant it sounds like 'c' in 'cat'

comer	*café*	*cupo*	*casa*	*clavo*
कोमेर	काफे	कूपो	कासा	क्लावो

ch (चे) like 'ch' in 'church'

mucho *ancho* *dicho* *muchacha*
मूचो आन्चो दीचो मूचाचा

d (दे) Like 'th' in 'though'

donde *pared* *sed* *vida*
दोन्दे पारेद सेद वीदा

f (एफ) Like 'f' in English

falta *francés* *dificil*
फाल्ता फ्रान्सेस दिफीसिल

g (खे or हे). Takes the sound of

(i) (ग) like 'g' in 'go', before 'a', 'o' and 'u' or a consonant.

gama *gustar* *góta* *gracia*
गामा गुस्तार गोता ग्रासिया

(ii) (ख) Before 'e' and 'f', it is pronounced as (ख)

gentle *general* *gitano*
खेन्ते खेनेराल खीतानो

(iii) Occurring before 'ur and 'u' it becomes गे (gue) or गी (gui) like in gate and guinea

guerra *águila*
गेर्रा आगीला

(iv) and followed by 'ue', g becomes 'गुए' like in antiguedad
आन्तिगुएदाद

h (आचे) **Always silent (Skip to the next sound)**

hacer	*hoy*	*ahora*
आसेर	ओई	आओरा

j (खोता) **Like the SPANISH (ख) in most parts of Spain**

juan	*Julio*	*lejos*
खुआन	खूलीयो	लेखोस

While in Latin American is sounds like ह

हुआन	हूनियो	लेहोस

k (का) **Like 'k' in English 'kilo'**

kilogramo	*kilómetro*
कीलोग्रामो	कीलोमेत्रो

l (एल) **Like 'l' in English 'alone'**

lejos	*isla*
लेहोस	ईस्ला

ll (एल्ये) **Like 'll' in English 'million' (in Latin American, it is pronounced like 'y' as in yam)**

calle	*llamar*	*valle*
काल्ये	ल्यामार	वाल्ये

m (एमे) **English 'm'**

mano	*mapa*	*importe*
मानो	मापा	इम्पोंते

n (एने) **English 'n'**

junio	*general*	*pan*	*negro*
खूनीयो	खेनेराल	पान	नेग्रो

ñ (एन्ये) **Like 'ni' in 'oniion'**

niño *señor* *pequeño* *año*
नीन्यो सेन्योर पेकेन्यो आन्यो

p (पे) Like English 'p'

poner *rápido* *possible* *tiempo*
पोनेर रापिदो पोसीब्ले तीयेम्पो

q Always found with 'u' and pronounced like'c' in 'cat' 'Qu' is always followed by 'e'e or 'i' and is pronounced like 'के' (Que) and 'की'(qui) in SPANISH.

r (एरे) A carefully pronounced English 'r'

rojo *rico* *río*
रोखो रीको रीयो

rr (एर्रे) A strongly rolled of trilled 'r'

arroz *arriba* *sierra* *irregular*
आर्रोस आर्रीबा सीएर्रा इर्रेगुलार

s (एसे) Like 's' in 'simple'

siglo *santo* *vista* *así*
सीग्लो सान्तो वीस्ता आसी

t (ते) Like SPANISH 'त'

patata *santo* *tener* *tinto*
पाताता सान्तो तेनेर तीन्तो

v (उवे) See 'b/v'

vivir *verde* *favor*
वीवीर वेर्दे फावोर

w (ऊवे दोब्ले) Like 'w' in English 'whiskey'. it is only found in foreign words take into Spanish.

Wagner *whiskey*
वागनेर विस्की

x (एकिस) (i) like 'gs' when it comes between vowels

examen *éxito*

एक्सामेन एक्सीतो

(ii) Like 's' before a consonant

explicar *extremo*

एसप्लीकार एसत्रेमो

y (य) As 'y' in 'young'

yo *ayudar* *mayor*

यो आयूदार मायोर

but occurring independently it is pronounced as the alphabet 'e' (ई) in English.

z (थे or स) Always like 'th' in 'thin' (with aspiration). (In Latin American like 's' in 'thus').

cruz *pobrezapaz* *pasar* *caza*

क्रूस पोर्बेसापास पासार कासा

Pronunciation Patterns (accents)

Spanish is pronounced in a rhythmic way and the rhythm is produced by two basic rules:

(a) If a word ends in a vowel (a, e, i, o, u_, -s or –n, the last but one vowel sound is stressed:

(carne)	- *Kaarnēe*	- कारने
(pluma)	- *ploomaa*	- पलूमा
(preciso)	- *prēesiso*	- प्रेसीसो
(señorita)	- *sēenyoriita*	- सेन्योरीता

(b) If a word ends in anything else (consonants), the last vowel sound is stressed:

(natural) - *nāatūraal* - नातूराल
(trabajar) - *ttraabākhaar* - त्राबाखार
(señor) - *sēenyor* - सेन्योर
(papel) - *paapēel* - पापेल
unless otherwise indicated with an caccent mark (').

The words that do not confirm to the rules given above bear a written accent mark (') over the stressed vowel:

(Américan) - *amēeriikaa* - अमेरीका
(Mécico) - *mēekhiiko* - मेथिको
(médico) - *mēediiko* - मेदिको
(jamás) - *khaamaas* - खामास
(árbol) - *aarbōle* - आरबोल
(religión) - *Rayleekhiyon* - रेलीयोओन

Punctuation

Spanish begins questions and exclamations with their respective punctuation marks inverted.
Dónde está el banco? (Where is the bank?)
dōn-day ās-taa l baanko- दान्दे एस्ता एल बाल्को
Qué edifico tan alto (What a tall building!)
k aidifisiio tāan aalto - के एदिफीसीओ तान आल्तो

English and Spanish punctuations are, in general, the same.

Capitalization

Spanish employee small letter for:

(a) Adjective of nationality:
el vino español (Spanish wine),
l beeno espāanyol एल बीनो एसपान्योल
las familias españolas (Spanish families)
laas fāamiiliyoos espāanyolaas –
लास फामिलियास एसपान्योलास

(b) Names of languages:
el inglés (English) *l inglace* - एल इनगलेस
el español (Spanish)*l espāanyol* - एल एसपाल्योल

(c) Names of days of the week, and months:
Lunes (Monday) - *loonēs*- लूनेस
miércoles (Tuesday) - *mearkolace* - मिएरकोलेस
sábado (Saturday) - *sāabāado* - साबादो
enero (January) - *enēero* - ऐनेरो
mayo (May) - *māayo*- मायो

(d) The pronoun 'I'
yo - *yō*- यो

Formation of a Spanish Sentence

Spanish leaves out words that we put in, puts in words that we leave out, arranges sentences differently, emphasises them differently and so on. Most of these differences will be explained to you in the course of your study, but some will never be explained because there is no clear explanation for them.

There are three important things to do in learning to pronounce Spanish words:

- Reading out the words exactly what is written.
- Repeating exactly what you read.
- Practicing the sounds aloud at every opportunity.

➢ Notice the differences between the pronunciation of Spanish & the prononciation of English.

1. Spanish & Spanish Americans speak alertly & fast, their words seem to be all in front of the month.

2. The intonation of the Spanish speech is different from the intonation of English speech. Every language has its own characteristic, intonations, so does Spanish.
3. The majority of Spanish syllables end in a vowel sound. This fact helps you make the difference between the Spanish pronunciation the English pronunciation of the following words.

Spanish Phonetic	English	English Phonetic	Spanish
↓	↓	↓	↓
Pro–fe–sor	Pro–fess-o	*profesō-o*	प्रोफेसोर
Ne-ce–sa–rio	Nec-e–ssar–y	*Nesesaariio*	नेसेसारियो

4. Vowels are short, sharp clear although Spanish vowels are sometimes hurried a little in unstressed syllables they are never given the sound of their vowels or left out altogether.

5. Spanish vowel is always a single, pure sound. The emphasis is purely on the vowels (a, e, i, o, u) that is not always true of English vowels.

6. Constants are sounded more lightly than in English.

One of the most important characteristies of Spanish language is that, there is great liberty in putting of the order of the sentence. But there are certain rules, which are required to be taken care of:

- Personal subject pronoun is not necessary to be written the endings of the verbs it selves but whom it refers to.
- Achieved are normally placed after the noun.
- In case of he/she personal subject is shown (EL/ELLA).
- For making a sentence negative we just put 'No' before verb in any case.
  No hablo español
  (I don't speak Spanish)
- For making a sentence interrogative we just put the interrogation signs on both the sides. This is one of the important & very rare quality of Spanish language.
  Hablas español?
  Do you speak Spanish?
  No hablas español?
  (Don't you speak Spanish)

- While making the sentence in the verb we just remove the last two letters of any particular verbs (as, er, is) & we add the conjugations of that respective verb.
  Hablar - Hablo - I speak
  Comer - Comes - You eat
  Vivir - Vivimos - You live
- Just to put the stress on any letter or to emphasize it we put out sign (‘) on the letter which is called account (acento).
  Médico
  Deficil
- Passive voice is less used

Conjugations of the verbs

Past

Present

Future

Present tense: -

ar ending verbs: -

Estudiar (To study)
Trabajar (To work)
Fumar (To smoke)
Hablar (To speak)
Llamar (To call)

Conjugation: -

Yo (I)	-	O	Nosotros (We)	-	amos
Tú (you)	-	as	Vosotros (you all)	-	áis
EL/LLA (He/She)	-	a	Ellos/Ellas (They)	-	an

er ending-

O	emos
es	éis
e	en

ir ending

O	imos
es	is
e	en

Past Tense

In Spanish there are two types of past tense, which is used according to the nature of the sentence.

Preterit - Imperfect

Preterit

ar ending

é	amos
aste	asteis
ó	aron

er & ir ending

í	imos
iste	isteis
ío	ierov

Imperfect

ar ending

aba	abamos
abas	abáis
aba	aban

er & ir ending

ía	iamos
ías	íais
ía	ían

Future Tense

In future tense unlike other tense the last two letters of the verbs (ar, er, ir) are not removed instead the conjugations are added after the verb & the conjugation is the same in the three types of verbs

é	amos
ás	abeis
á	an

Hablar - Hablaré
(I will speak)
Comer - comeré
(I will eat)
Escribir- Escribiré
(I will write)

Subject = First person, Singular number

1. I go.
Vov
Bo ̈i
बोइ

2. I am going.
Estoy yendo
Ēstōi yendō
एस्तोई येन्दो

3. I have gone.
He ido
ē üdo
ए ईदो

4. I have been going.

He sido yendo
ē udōyendō
ए सिदो येन्दो

5. I went.
Fui
Fooi
फुई

6. I was going.
Estuve yendo
ēstoobēe yendō
एसतूबे येन्दो

7. I had gone.
Yo había ido
yō aabiyvā üdo
यो आबिया इदो

8. I had been going.
Yo había sido yendo
yō aabiyā cido yendō
यो आबिया सिदो योनदो

9. I will go.
Iré
iiray

इरे

10. I will be going .
    Yo habría ido
    yō aabriyā iido
    यो आब्रिया इदो

11. I will have gone
    yo habré ido
    yō aabrē iido
    यो आब्रे इदो

12. I can go.
    Puedo ir
    poeedo iir
    पुएदो ईर

13. I could go.
    Podria ir.
    pōdrria iir
    पोद्रिया ईर

14. I will be able to go.
    Podré ir
    pōdray iir
    पोद्रे ईर

15. Can I go?
Puedo ir yo?
pooedo iir yō
पुएदो ईर यो ?

16. Could I go?
Podría ir yo?
pōdraia iir yō ?
पोद्रिया ईर यो ?

17. Will I be able to go?
Podré ir yo?
pōdray iir yō
पोद्रे ईर यो ?

18. I want to go.
Ouiero ir
kiēro iir
केरिया इर ?

19. I wanted to go.
Queriá ir
kayria iir
केरिया इर ?

20. I would like to go.

Me gustaría ir.
mēe goostāriya iir
मे गुस्तारिया इर ?

21. I should go/ I must go/ I ought to go.
Debré ir/ Debo ir/ debo de ir
dēebray iir / dēebo iir / Dēebo dē iir
देब्रे इर / देबो इर / देबो दे इर

Grammar

Tense

Past (Pasado)	Present (Presente)	Future (Futuro)
I went (Fui)	I go (voy)	I will go (iré)
fooii - फुई	*Boii* – बोई	*iroay* - इरे
You went (Fuiste)	You go (vas)	You will go (irás)
fooiiste - फुईस्ते	*bāas* - बास	*iiraas* - इरास
He went ((Fue)	He goes (Va)	He will go (irá)
fooee - फुए	*Bā* - बा	*iiraa* - इरा
We went (Fuimos)	We go (Vamos)	We will go (iramos)
fooiimōos - फुईमोस	*Baamos* - बामोस	*iiraamōs* - इरामोस
You all went (Fuistus)	You all go (Váis)	You all will go(iráis)
fooisteyis - फुईस्तेईस	*Baais* - बाइस	*îirāais* - इराइस
They went (Fueron)	They go (van)	They will go (irán)
fooeroon - फुएरोन	*Baan* - बान	*iirāan* - ईरान

A Review of Spanish Verbs

Like wise in their languages Spanish too has got two types of verbs: -

Regular	**Irregular**
Hablar (To speak)	Poder (To be able to)
AAblaar - आबलार	*pōdēer* - पोदेर
Cantar (To sing)	Hacer (To do)
Kaantaar - काबतार	*AAsēr* - आसेर
Escribir (To write)	Jugar (To play)
acekribiir - एसक्रीबीर	*Khoogaar* - खुगार
	Ir (To go)
	iir - ईर

In Spanish the verbs are identified in a totally different way unlike other languages. All Spanish verbs always end up in three ways: -

ar

er

ir

These are respectively called –

Hablar	-ar ending verbs
Comer	-er ending verbs
Vivir	-ir ending verbs

Irregular verbs here too in Spanish have got different treatment like other languages.

Subject Pronoun

Singular	Plural
I (yo)	We (nosotros)
yō - यो	*nosōtrōs* - नोसीत्रोस
You (tú)	You all (vosotros)
tōo - तू	vosōtrōs - नोसोत्रोस

He/she (Ėl/ella/vd.)	They (ellos/ellas/vds.)
Él - l - एल	āeyos - एयोस
lya - एल्या	āeyaas - एयास
oosted - उस्तेद	oostedes - उस्तेदेस

Note: vd & vds forms of subject pronoun here are for representing formal form of you & you all respectively.

Note: In Spanish it's always not important to mention out the subject pronoun because the conjugation itself of every pronoun is different & clearly inficates whom it refers to.

For example:-

(yo) hablo espanal *yō aablo ēespanyol* - यो आबलो एस्पान्योल
(I speak Spanish)

(Ėl) canta una cancion e*l kanta oona kausiōn* - एल कान्ता उना कानसिओन
(He sings a song)

1. To abscond = Fugarse = *foogāarse* = फूगारसे

2. To absorb = Absorber = *aabrsōrsē* = आबसोरबेर
3. To accept = Aceptar = *aacēptaar* = आसेपतार
4. To accompany = Acompañar = *aakompanyaar* = आकोम्पान्यार
5. To act = Actuar = *aaktūaar* = आक्तूआर
6. To add = Añadir = *aanyādiir* = आन्यादीर
7. To admire = Admirar = *aadmiiraar* = आदमीरार
8. To advise = Consejar = *kōnsekhār* = कोन्सेरबार
9. To agree = Acordarse = *aakōrdaarsē* = आकोरदारसे
10. To allow = Permitir = *pēmiitiir* = पेरमीतिर
11. To apologize = Disculparse = *diiskūlpāarse* = दिसकुलपारसे
12. To apply = Solicitar = *sōoliicitāar* = सोलिसितार
13. To approach = Acercarse = *aasēerkāarse* = आसेरकारसे
14. To arise = Surgir = *soorkhiir* = सुरखीर
15. To arrange = Arreglar = *aarēglāar* = आरेगलार
16. To arrive = Llegar = *yēgāar* = येगार
17. To ask = Pedir = *pēediir* = पेदीर
18. To assist = Ayudar = *aayudāar* = आयुदार

19.	To assure	=	Asegurar	=	*aaseegooräar*	=	आसेगुरार
20.	To attach	=	Adjuntar	=	*aadkhoontaar*	=	आदखुनतार
21.	To attack	=	Atacar	=	*atakäar*	=	आताकार
22.	To attempt	=	Tratar	=	*traa-taar*	=	त्रातार
23.	To attend	=	Asistir	=	*aasiistiir*	=	आसीसतीर
24.	To attract	=	Atraer	=	*aa-traer*	=	आत्रार
25.	To authorize	=	Autotizar	=	*aaootōriisäar*	=	आऊतोरिसार
26.	To awake	=	Despertarse	=	*Dēespēertäarse*	=	देसपेरतारसे
27.	To able	=	Poder	=	*pōdēer*	=	पोदेर
28.	To ban	=	Prohibir	=	*proiibiir*	=	प्रोईबीर
29.	To bargain	=	Regatear	=	*raygätēaar*	=	रेगातेआर
30.	To bath	=	Bañarse	=	*baanyarse*	=	बान्यारसे
31.	To batter	=	Rebozar	=	*rēebosaar*	=	रेबोसार
32.	To beat	=	Golpear	=	*gōlpēeaar*	=	गोलपेआर
33.	To befriend	=	Hacerse amigo	=	*aasērsē aamigō*	=	आसेर से आमीगो
34.	To beg	=	Mendigar	=	*mēendiigäar*	=	मेन्दिगार
35.	To begin	=	Empezar	=	*ēmpēesäar*	=	एमपेसार

36.	To behave	=	Comportar	=	*kompōrtaar*	=	कोमपोरतार
37.	To believe	=	Creer	=	*krēer*	=	क्रेर
38.	To bend	=	Curbar	=	*kurbāar*	=	कुरबार
39.	To betray	=	Traicionar	=	*Trāiiciionāar*	=	त्राईसियोनार
40.	To bid	=	Pujar	=	*pookhāar*	=	पुखार
41.	To bite	=	Morder	=	*mōrēer*	=	मोरदेर
42.	To blast	=	Bombardear	=	*bombāardear*	=	बोम्बारदेआर
43.	To bless	=	Bendicionar	=	*bēendiicionāar*	=	बेन्दीसियोनार
44.	To block	=	Bloquear	=	*Blokeār*	=	ब्लोकेयार
45.	To blossom	=	Floreceer	=	*flow-re-sēr*	=	फलोरेसेर
46.	To blow	=	Soplar	=	*sōplāar*	=	सोपलार
47.	To bolt	=	Cerrar	=	*sērāar*	=	सेरार
48.	To bore	=	Perforar	=	*pēerforāar*	=	पेरफोरार
49.	To bounce	=	Remoter	=	*rēmotēer*	=	रेमोतेर
50.	To break	=	Romper	=	*rōmpēer*	=	रोमपेर
51.	To breath	=	Respirar	=	*Rēespiirāar*	=	रेसपीरार
52.	To brush	=	Cepillarse	=	*sēepiyaarsēe*	=	सेपिल्यारसे

53.	To buy	=	Comprar	=	*kōmprāar*	=	कोमप्रार
54.	To calculate	=	Calcular	=	*kalkōōlāar*	=	कालकूलार
55.	To call	=	Llamar	=	*yāamēar*	=	यामार
56.	To cancel	=	Cancelar	=	*kanselāar*	=	कानसेलार
57.	To care	=	Cuidar	=	*kuiidāar*	=	कूईदार
58.	To carry	=	Llevar	=	*yēevāar*	=	ल्येवार
59.	To cash	=	Cobrar	=	*kobrāar*	=	कोब्रार
60.	To catch	=	Coger	=	*kokher*	=	कोखेर
61.	To certify	=	Certificar	=	*sērtiifiikāar*	=	सेरतीफिकार
62.	To change	=	Cambiar	=	*kāambiiār*	=	कामबिआर
63.	To chase	=	Perseguir	=	*pēerseguiir*	=	पेरसेगीर
64.	To cheat	=	Engañar	=	*ēm-gāa-nyaar*	=	एनगान्यार
65.	To check	=	Chequear	=	*chēekēyāar*	=	चेकेयार
66.	To choke	=	Ahogar	=	*aaogāar*	=	आओगार
67.	To chop	=	Cortar algo en pedazos	=	*aalgō ēn pēdāasōs kortār*	=	आलगो एन कोरतार देदासोस
68.	To choose	=	Elegir	=	*ēlēkhiir*	=	एलेखीर
69.	To chuckle	=	Reirse entre	=	*rēeiirsēe ēntrēe*	=	रेईरसे एन्त्रे

			dientes		*dieentēs*		दिएतेस
70.	To circulate	=	Circular	=	*siirkoolāar*	=	सिरकुलार
71.	To claim	=	Reclamar	=	*rēcklamāar*	=	रेक्लामार
72.	To clap	=	Aplaudir	=	*aaplaoodiir*	=	आपलाऊदीर
73.	To clean	=	Limpiar	=	*Liimpiiar*	=	लिमपीआर
74.	To clerch	=	Apretar	=	*āaprēetāar*	=	आप्रेतार
75.	To close	=	Cerrar	=	*sēerāar*	=	सेरार
76.	To collect	=	Coleccionar	=	*kolekcionāar*	=	कोलेकसियोनार
77.	To combine	=	Combinar	=	*kombiinaar*	=	कोमबीनार
78.	To come	=	Venir	=	*Bēniir*	=	बेनीर
79.	To compel	=	Obligar	=	*ōbliigaar*	=	आब्लोगार
80.	To complain	=	Quejarse	=	*kekhaarse*	=	केखारसे
81.	To confide	=	Confiar	=	*kōnfiiāar*	=	कोनफिआर
82.	To confirm	=	Confirmar	=	*kōnfiirmāar*	=	कोनफिमार
83.	To contain	=	Contener	=	*kōntēnēer*	=	कोनतेनेर
84.	To control	=	Controlar	=	*kōntrōlāar*	=	कोनत्रोलार
85.	To cover	=	Cubrir	=	*koobriir*	=	कुब्रीर

86. To cry = Llorar = *yōrāar* = योरार
87. To cure = Curar = *koorāar* = कुरार
88. To cut = Cortar = *kōrtāar* = कोरतार
89. To damage = Dañar = *dāanyaar* = दान्यार
90. To dance = Bailar = *baiilāar* = बाईलार
91. To dare = Desafiar = *Dēesāafiiar* = देसाफिआर
92. To decay = Pudrirse = *poodriirse* = पूदरीरसे
93. To decide = Decidir = *Dēsiidiir* = देसिदीर
94. To declare = Declarar = *Dēklārāar* = देकलारार
95. To deferd = Defender = *Dēfēndēer* = देफेनदेर
96. To dehydrate = Deshidratar = *Dēsiidrāatāar* = देसइद्रातार
97. To delay = Tardar = *Tāaradāar* = तारदार
98. To deliver = Repartir = *Rēepāartiir* = रेपारतीर
99. To demand = Exigir = *Ēksiikhiir* = एक्सीखीर
100. To demolish = Derribar = *Deribaar* = देरीबीर
101. To depart = Salir = *Salir* = सलीर
102. To describe = Describir = *Deskribir* = देसक्रिबीर
103. To desire = Desear = *De-seaar* = देसेआर

104. To die = Morir = *Môrir* = मोरिर
105. To dig = Cabar = *Cäbar* = काबार
106. To dip = Meter = *Meter* = मेतेर
107. To disagree = Discrepar = *Diskrapar* = दीसक्रेपार
108. To discolour = Descolorer = *Daskôlorar* = देसकोलोरार
109. To disinfect = Desenfetar = *Dasenphetar* = देसेन्फेतार
110. To dislike = Odiar = *Ôdiar* = ओदीआर
111. To display = Mostrar = *Môstrar* = मोसत्रार
112. To distribute = Distribuir = *Distribûir* = दीसत्रीबुईर
113. To do = Hacer = *acer* = आसेर
114. To donote = Donar = *Dōanar* = दोनार
115. To dream = Soñar = *Sōnyar* = सोन्यार
116. To drink = Beber = *Beber* = बेबेर
117. To dribble = Gotear = *Gotaer* = गोनेआर
118. To drop = Dejar caer = *Dekhaar kaaer* = देखार काऐर
119. To dry = Secar = *Secar* = सेकार
120. To dye = Teñir = *Tenyir* = तेन्यीर

121. To eat = Comer = *Comer* = कोमेर
122. To educate = Educar = *edûcar* = एदुकार
123. To elect = Elegir = *eligir* = एलीखीर
124. To embarrass = Avergonzar = *aver-gon-saar* = आबेरगुएन्सार
125. To emigrate = Emigrar = *emigrar* = एमीगरार
126. To encourage = Animar = *animar* = आनीमार
127. To enjoy = Gozar = *Gôzar* = गोसार
128. To enter = Entrar = *entrar* = एंतरार
129. To erase = Borrar = *borraar* = बोर्रार
130. To err = Errar = *arar* = एररार
131. To escape = Escapar = *askāpār* = एसकापार
132. To exhibit = Exhibir = *ex-iibiir* = एक्सअीबीर
133. To expedite = Acelerar = *acelerar* = आसेलेरार
134. To fail = Fracasar = *phrakāsār* = फ्राकारसार
135. To faint = Desmayarse = *dasmayarse* = देसमायारसे
136. To fall = Caer = *caer* = काएर
137. To fasten = Atar = *ātār* = आतार
138. To fear = Temer = *temar* = देमेर

139. To feed	=	Alimentar	=	*Ālimentār*	=	आलीमेन्तार
140. To fight	=	Luchar	=	*lōochār*	=	लुचार
141. To filter	=	Filtrar	=	*philtrār*	=	फिलतरार
142. To finish	=	Acabar	=	*akābâr*	=	आकाबार
143. To flee	=	Huir	=	*ōōir*	=	ऊईर
144. To flow	=	Fluir	=	*phtūir*	=	फलुईर
145. To fly	=	Volar	=	*bôlār*	=	बोलार
146. To forfeit	=	Decomiosar	=	*dakômisār*	=	देकोमीसार
147. To forget	=	Olvidar	=	*ōlbidār*	=	ओलबीदार
148. To forgive	=	Perdonar	=	*pardônār*	=	पेरदोनार
149. To frighten	=	Asustar	=	*Āsûstār*	=	आसुसतार
150. To gamble	=	Jugar	=	*Khugār*	=	खुगार
151. To get	=	Conseguir	=	*kônsaghir*	=	कोनसेगीर
152. To go	=	Ir	=	*Ir*	=	ईर
153. To guard	=	Proteger	=	*Protejer*	=	प्रोतेखेर
154. To guide	=	Guiar	=	*Guiār*	=	गीआर
155. To hang	=	Colgar	=	*kôlgār*	=	कोलगार

156. To harm = Perjudicar = *perkhurdikar* = पेरखुरदीफार
157. To haste = Odiar = *ōodiār* = ओदीआर
158. To heat = Calentar = *kalentār* = कालेनतार
159. To help = Ayudar = *Āiûdār* = आयूदार
160. To hide = Esconder = *eskondar* = एसकोनदेर
161. To hit = Pegar = *pegār* = पेगार
162. To hold = Aguantar = *Āgûntār* = आगुनतार
163. To honour = Honrar = *ônrār* = ओनरार
164. To hug = Abrazar = *Ābrasār* = आबरासार
165. To hurt = Herir = *arir* = एरीर
166. To hypnotise = Hipnotizar = *Iptōnisar* = इपतोनीसार
167. To identify = Identificar = *identiphikar* = इदेनतीफीकार
168. To ignore = Ignorar = *Ignōrār* = इगनोरार
169. To imagine = Imaginar = *Imajinār* = इमाखीनार
170. To import = Importar = *Impōtār* = इम्पोरतार
171. To improve = Mejorar = *Mejorār* = मेखोरार
172. To include = Incluir = *Inclûir* = इनक्लूईर
173. To indicate = Indicar = *Indikār* = इनदीकार

174.	To influence	=	Influir	=	*Inphuîir*	=	इनफ्लूईर
175.	To insist	=	Insistir	=	*Insîstir*	=	इनसीसतीर
176.	To insure	=	Asegurar	=	*āsegurār*	=	असेगुरार
177.	To interrupt	=	Interrumpir	=	*Intārompir*	=	इनतेरूमपीर
178.	To intimate	=	Insinuar	=	*Insinuār*	=	इनसीनुआर
179.	To introduce	=	Introducir	=	*Introdûcir*	=	इनत्रोदुसीर
180.	To irrigate	=	Irrigar	=	*Irigar*	=	इरीगार
181.	To join	=	Unir	=	*Ōonir*	=	ऊनीर
182.	To joke	=	Hablar enbroma	=	*Āblār anbrōmaa*	=	आबलार एनब्रोमा
183.	To judge	=	Juzgar	=	*khaosgaer*	=	खुसगार
184.	To jump	=	Saltar	=	*sāltār*	=	सालतार
185.	To keep	=	Guardar	=	*gūardār*	=	गुआरदार
186.	To kiss	=	Bezar	=	*Besär*	=	बेसार
187.	To kneel	=	Arrodellarse	=	*ārôdellārse*	=	आररोदेनयारसे
188.	To knock	=	Laamar la puerta	=	*ll a mār la puarta*	=	ल्यामार ला पुएरता

189.	To know	=	Saber	=	*Sāber*	=	साबेर
190.	To lack	=	Faltar	=	*Phaltār*	=	फालतार
191.	To land	=	Aterrizar	=	*ātarisār*	=	आतेरीसार
192.	To laugh	=	Reir	=	*Reir*	=	रेईर
193.	To lay	=	Poner	=	*Poner*	=	पोनेर
194.	To lead	=	Dirigir	=	*Dirigîr*	=	दीरीखीर
195.	To leak	=	Gotear	=	*Gotaer*	=	गोतेआर
196.	To leap	=	Saltar	=	*sāltār*	=	सालतार
197.	To leave	=	Salir	=	*Saalir*	=	सालीर
198.	To lecture	=	Dar clases	=	*dāar klāsas*	=	दार क्लासेस
199.	To lend	=	Prestar	=	*prestāar*	=	प्रेसतार
200.	To lift	=	Levantar	=	*lavāantār*	=	लेवान्तार
201.	To like	=	Gustar	=	*Gōostār*	=	गुस्तार
202.	To live	=	Vivir	=	*Viviir*	=	बीबीर
203.	To look	=	Mirar	=	*Mirāar*	=	मीरार
204.	To loosen	=	Aflojar	=	*aphlojār*	=	आपलोखार
205.	To love	=	Amar	=	*aamār*	=	आमार
206.	To lubricate	=	Lubricar	=	*lûbricār*	=	लुबरीकार

207.	To mail	=	Mandar por correo	=	*Māandār pôr côrrlo*	= मानदार पोर कोरयो
208.	To make	=	Hacer	=	*acer*	= आसेर
209.	To maltreat	=	Maltratar	=	*Māaltratar*	= मालतरातार
210.	To marry	=	Casarse	=	*kāasārse*	= कासारसे
211.	To mash	=	Machacar	=	*māachakār*	= माचाक़ार
212.	To massage	=	Dar mensajes	=	*dār mensājes*	= दार मेन्साखेस
213.	To measure	=	Medir	=	*mediir*	= मेदीर
214.	To meet	=	Encontrar	=	*ankontrār*	= एन्कोन्तार
215	To misguide	=	Equivocar	=	*aquibôkār*	= एकीबोकार
216.	To miss	=	Perder	=	*perder*	= पेरदेर
217.	To misunderstand	=	Comprender mal	=	*cômprender māal*	= कोमप्रेन्देर माल
218.	To mix	=	Mezclar	=	*mesiklaar*	= मेस्कलार
219.	To nag	=	Molestar	=	*môlestār*	= मोलेसतार
220.	To nap	=	Echar la siesta	=	*achār laa siestā*	= ऐचार ला सिएसता
221.	To need	=	Necesitar	=	*nececitār*	= नेसेसीतार

222.	To notify	=	Notificar	=	*nôtifikār*	=	नोतीफीकार
223.	To obey	=	Obedecer	=	*ôbedecer*	=	ओबेदेसेर
224.	To observe	=	Observar	=	*ôbserbār*	=	ओबसेबार
225.	To obtain	=	Obtenter	=	*ôbtener*	=	ओबतेनेर
226.	To occupy	=	Ocupar	=	*ôcûpār*	=	ओकुपार
227.	To offer	=	Ofrecer	=	*ôfrecer*	=	ओफरेसेर
228.	To ooze	=	Sudar	=	*sûdār*	=	सुदार
229.	To open	=	Abrir	=	*Ābrīr*	=	आबरीर
230.	To order	=	Ordernar	=	*ôrdernōr*	=	ओरदेरनार
231.	To organize	=	Organizar	=	*orgānisār*	=	ओरगानीसार
232.	To overflow	=	Derramarse	=	*darramaarse*	=	देररामारसे
233.	To overload	=	Sobrecargar	=	*sôbrecârgāar*	=	सोबरेकारगार
234.	To overtake	=	Adelantar	=	*âdelentār*	=	आदेलान्तार
235.	To own	=	Poseer	=	*pôser*	=	पोसीर
236.	To pacify	=	Tranquilizar	=	*trānkilisār*	=	त्रान्कीलीसार
237.	To paint	=	Pintar	=	*pintār*	=	पीन्तार
238.	To pass	=	Pasar	=	*pâsār*	=	पासार
239.	To pay	=	Pagar	=	*pâgār*	=	पागार

240. To peal = Pelar = *pelaar* = पेलार
241. To persuade = Convencer = *konvenser* = कोनबेन्सेर
242. To play = Jugar = *khugaar* = खुगार
243. To plead = Rogar = *rôgār* = रोगार
244. To pray = Rezar = *resār* = रेसार
245. To prepare = Praparar = *prapārār* = प्रेपारार
246. To produce = Producir = *prôdụ̂cir* = प्रोदुसीर
247. To purchase = Comprar = *cômprār* = कोमप्रार
248. To push = Empujar = *ampûjār* = एमपुखार
249. To question = Preguntar = *preguntār* = प्रेगुन्तार
250. To rain = Llover = *yober* = योबेर
251. To reach = Llegar = *yegār* = येगार
252. To read = Leer = *lēer* = लेएर
253. To reduce = Reducir = *radûcir* = रेदुसीर
254. To regret = Lamentar = *lāamentār* = लामेन्तार
255. To reject = Rechazar = *rechasār* = रेचासार
256. To relax = Relajar = *ralāajār* = रेलाखार

257.	To relieve	=	Aliviar	=	*āliviār*	=	आलीबीआर
258.	To repair	=	Reparar	=	*rapârār*	=	रेपारार
259.	To repeat	=	Repitir	=	*rêpitir*	=	रेपीतीर
260.	To reply	=	Responder	=	*respônder*	=	रेसपोन्देर
261.	To report	=	Informar	=	*infôrmār*	=	इन्फोरमार
262.	To rescue	=	Rescatar	=	*rascatār*	=	रेसकातार
263.	To rest	=	Escansar	=	*ascansar*	=	एसकानसार
264.	To return	=	Volver	=	*bôlbar*	=	बोल्बेर
265.	To ride	=	Montar	=	*mōontār*	=	मोन्तार
266.	To rise	=	Subir	=	*Sûbir*	=	सुबीर
267.	To roar	=	Bramar	=	*Brāmār*	=	ब्रामार
268.	To roast	=	Tostar	=	*tòstār*	=	तोसतार
269.	To rub	=	Frotar	=	*phrotār*	=	फ्रोतार
270.	To run	=	Correr	=	*korrer*	=	कोररेर
271.	To rush	=	Hacer la prisa	=	*acer laa prisa*	=	आसेर ला प्रीसा
272.	To sacrifice	=	Sacrificar	=	*sakrificār*	=	साकरीफीकार
273.	To sanction	=	Sancionar	=	*sancîonār*	=	सेनसयोनार
274.	To satisfy	=	Satisfacher	=	*satisphācher*	=	सातीसफाचेर

275.	To save	=	Ahorrar	=	*āorrār*	=	अओररार
276.	To say	=	Decir	=	*decir*	=	देसीर
277.	To scatter	=	Esparcir	=	*asparciir*	=	एसपारसीर
278.	To scratch	=	Arañar	=	*âranar*	=	आरान्यार
279.	To cream	=	Chillar	=	*chiyār*	=	चीयार
280.	To search	=	Buscar	=	*Buskār*	=	बुसकार
281.	To see	=	Ver	=	*Vêr*	=	बेर
282.	To seek	=	Buscar	=	*Bûskār*	=	बुसकार
283.	To sell	=	Vender	=	*vender*	=	बेन्देर
284.	To select	=	Seleceionar	=	*sālekcionār*	=	सेलेकसीओनार
285.	To separate	=	Seperar	=	*sāparār*	=	सेपेरार
286.	To shake	=	Temblar	=	*tāmblār*	=	तेमबलार
287.	To share	=	Compartir	=	*compārtiir*	=	कोमपारतीर
288.	To shatter	=	Romper	=	*rompār*	=	रोमपेर
289.	To shrink	=	Encoger	=	*āncogar*	=	एनकोखेर
290.	To shut	=	Cerrar	=	*cerrar*	=	सेरार
291.	To sing	=	Cantar	=	*cântār*	=	कोनतार

No.	English		Spanish		Pronunciation		Hindi
292.	To sink	=	Hundir	=	*Ûndiir*	=	उन्दीर
293.	To sit	=	Sentarse	=	*saantărsā*	=	सेनतारसे
294.	To slap	=	Abofetear	=	*abôphetaār*	=	अबोफेतायासे
295.	To sleep	=	Dormir	=	*dôrmir*	=	दोरमीर
296.	To slip	=	Caer	=	*coer*	=	काएर
297.	To smell	=	Oler	=	*Ôlar*	=	ओलर
298.	To snatch	=	Interntar	=	*intarntăr*	=	इनतेरतार
299.	To speak	=	Hablar	=	*āblār*	=	आबलार
300.	To spit	=	Escupir	=	*ascupīr*	=	एसकुपीर
301.	To spoil	=	Estropear	=	*astropaār*	=	एसत्रोपेआर
302.	To spray	=	Atomizer	=	*atômisar*	=	उतोमीसेर
303.	To spread	=	Extender	=	*eks tenderr*	=	एकसतेनदेर
304.	To stab	=	Acuchillar	=	*acûchiyār*	=	आकुचीयार
305.	To stain	=	Remover	=	*ramobār*	=	रेमोबेर
306.	To stand	=	Estar de pie	=	*astār dā pîe*	=	एसतार दे पीए
307.	To stare	=	Mirar fijamente	=	*miirār phikhamênte*	=	मीरार फीखामेन्ते
308.	To start	=	Empezar	=	*empesār*	=	एमपेसार

309. To stay = Quedar = *kedār* = केदार
310. To steal = Robar = *rôbār* = रोबार
311. To stop = Parar = *pârār* = पारार
312. To store = Almacenar = *âlmâcenār* = अलमासेनार
313. To stretch = Estirar = *aasitirar* = एसतीरार
314. To suck = Sorber = *sôrbar* = सोरबेर
315. To suffer = Sufrir = *Sûfrīr* = सुफरीर
316. To surprise = Sorprender = *Sôrprender* = सोरप्रेन्देर
317. To surrender = Rendir = *rāndīr* = रेन्दीर
318. To swell = Hincarse = *incarse* = इन्कारसे
319. To tackle = Abordar = *âbordāar* = आबोरदार
320. To tag = Etiquetar = *eti-ketaar* = एतीकेतार
321. To take = Sacar = *sakār* = साकार
322. To talk = Hablar = *âblār* = आबलार
323. To tap = Golpear = *Golpear* = गोलपेसार
324. To tape = Recorder = *recôrdār* = रकोरदेर
325. To tattoo = Tatuar = *Tatûār* = तातुआर

326.	To teach	=	Enseñar	=	*anseñar*	=	एनसेन्यार
327.	To tear	=	Rasgar	=	*rasgār*	=	रासगार
328.	To terrorise	=	Aterorigar	=	*atarôrigār*	=	आतेरोरीगार
329.	To testify	=	Atestiguar	=	*atestigiiār*	=	अतेसतीगुआर
330.	To thank	=	Agradecer	=	*agradacer*	=	अग्रादेसेर
331.	To think	=	Pensar	=	*pensār*	=	पेनसार
332.	To throw	=	Echar	=	*achār*	=	ऐचार
333.	To tie	=	Atar	=	*atār*	=	आतार
334.	To tolerate	=	Tolerar	=	*tolarār*	=	तोलेरार
335.	To torture	=	Torturar	=	*tortûrār*	=	तारतुरार
336.	To touch	=	Tocar	=	*Tôcār*	=	तोकार
337.	To translate	=	Traducir	=	*trāducîr*	=	त्रारदुसीर
338.	To tremble	=	Temblar	=	*trāmblār*	=	त्रेमबलार
339.	To trim	=	Recortar	=	*racôrtār*	=	रेकोरतार
340.	To trust	=	Confiar	=	*Cônphiār*	=	कोन्फीयार
341.	To try	=	Tratar de	=	*Trâtār de*	=	तारतार दे
342.	To turn	=	Doblar	=	*dôblār*	=	दोबलार
343.	To type	=	Mecanografia	=	*macānografiar*	=	मेकोनोग्राफीआर

r

344.	To understand	=	Entender	=	*antendêr*	=	इनतेन्देर
345.	To undress	=	Desnudarse	=	*dasnûdarse*	=	देसनुदार से
346.	To unite	=	Juntar	=	*khûntār*	=	खुनतार
347.	To unload	=	Descargar	=	*Descargār*	=	देसकारगार
348.	To unlock	=	Abrir	=	*ābrîr*	=	आबरीर
349.	To upset	=	Trastonar	=	*trāstônār*	=	त्रासतोनार
350.	To use	=	Usar	=	*ûsār*	=	ऊसार
351.	To vacate	=	Dejar	=	*dekhār*	=	देखार
352.	To vary	=	Variar	=	*variār*	=	बारीआर
353.	To violate	=	Violar	=	*violar*	=	बीओलार
354.	To vote	=	Votar	=	*vôtar*	=	बोतार
355.	To wait	=	Esperar	=	*asperār*	=	एसपेरार
356.	To wake	=	Despertar	=	*des-per taar*	=	देसपेरतार
357.	To walk	=	Andar	=	*Ândār*	=	आनदार
358.	To wander	=	Dar una vuelta	=	*Dâr ûna Vûelta*	=	दार ऊना बुएल्ता

359. To warm = Calentarse = *kalêntārse* = कालेनतारसे
360. To wash = Lavar = *Lavāar* = लाबार
361. To waste = Perder = *perdēr* = पेरदेर
362. To watch = Mirar = *mirâr* = मीरार
363. To wave = Agitar = *akhitar* = अखीतार
364. To weigh = Pesar = *Pêsār* = पेसार
365. To whip = Azotar = *asotār* = असोतार
366. To whisper = Susurrar = *sûsûrrar* = सुसुरार
367. To whistle = Silbar = *silbar* = सीलबार
368. To wink = Hacer un duiño = *acar ûn duiño* = आसर ऊन दुईन्यो
369. To withdraw = Retirar = *rêtirār* = रेतीरार
370. To work = Trabajar = *trabakhâr* = त्राबारवार
371. To worry = Preocuparse = *preocûpārse* = प्रेओकुपारसे
372. To write = Escribir = *ascribir* = एसक्रीबीर

Nouns

1.	Account	=	La cuenta	=	*laa cooentaa*	=	ला कूएन्ता
2.	Acid	=	El ácido	=	*l aasido*	=	एल आसिदो
3.	Actor	=	El actor	=	*l aaktor*	=	एल आकतोर
4.	Address	=	La direccción	=	*laa direk-si-on*	=	ला दीरेक्सीओन
5.	Advertisement	=	El anuncio	=	*l aamoonsioo*	=	एल आनुनसीओ
6.	Agriculture	=	El agricóla	=	*l aagreekola*	=	एल आग्रीकोला
7.	Anger	=	La ira	=	*laa ira*	=	ला ईरा
8.	Animal	=	El bestia	=	*l bestiia*	=	एल बेसतीया
9.	Ankle	=	El tobillo	=	*l toebiyo*	=	एल तोबियो
10.	Answer	=	La respuesta	=	*laa reaspooastaa*	=	ला रेसपूएस्ता
11.	Apology	=	La oisculpa	=	*laa deeskoolpa*	=	ला दिसकुल्पा

12. Arch	=	El arco	=	*l aarko*	=	एल आरको
13. Arm	=	Brazo	=	*l braaso*	=	एल ब्रासो
14. Armpit	=	La axila	=	*laa aakseila*	=	ला आक्जीला
15. Baby	=	La niña	=	*laa neenya*	=	एल नीन्या
16. Bachelor	=	El soltero	=	*l soleteero*	=	एल सोलतेरो
17. Back	=	La espalda	=	*laspaalda*	=	ला एसपाल्दा
18. Backbone	=	La columna	=	*lcoloomnaa*	=	ला कोलून्मा
19. Backyard	=	El patio	=	*lpaatiiyo*	=	एल पाताओ
20. Banana	=	El plátano	=	*lplaataano*	=	एल प्लातानो
21. Beard	=	la barba	=	*laa baarba*	=	ला बारबा
22. Bed	=	La cama	=	*laa Kama*	=	ला कामा
23. Blister	=	La ampolla	=	*laa aampoya*	=	ला आमपोया
24. Blood	=	La sangre	=	*laa saangrey*	=	ला सान्ग्रे
25. Belly	=	El vientre	=	*l beyintre*	=	एल बेइन्त्रे
26. Book	=	El libro	=	*l leebro*	=	एल लीब्रो
27. Boy	=	El chico	=	*l cheeko*	=	एल चीको
28. Brain	=	La mente	=	*laa mainte*	=	ला मेन्ते
29. Bride	=	La novia	=	*laa noveeya*	=	ला नोबीया
30. Bug	=	El insecto	=	*l insectoe*	=	एल इनसेक्टो

31. Butter = La mantequilla = *laa maantekiya* = ला मान्तेकीया
32. Cabbage = El repollo = *l reepoyo* = एल रेपोयो
33. Calf = El ternero = *l tēernero* = एल तेरनेरो
34. Camel = El camello = *l cameyo* = एल कामेयो
35. Cap = El sombrero = *l sombrero* = एल सोमब्रेरो
36. Carpet = La alfombra = *laa aalfombraa* = ला आलफोम्ब्रा
37. Carrot = La zanahoria = *laa saanahoriya* = ला सानाहोरिया
38. Chair = La silla = *laa silya* = ला सील्या
39. Chameleon = El camaleón = *l kamaleeon* = एल कामालेओन
40. Cheek = La mejilla = *laa meekhilya* = ला मेखिल्या
41. Chest = El pecho = *l pēcho* = एल पेचो
42. Citizen = El ciudadano = *l siyudaadano* = एल सियूदादानों
43. Coal = El carbón = *l kaarbone* = एल कारबोन
44. Coast = La costa = *laa Kostaa* = ला कोस्ता
45. Coin = La moneda = *laa moneeda* = ला मोनेदा
46. Colour = El color = *l kolor* = एल कोलोर
47. Corner = El rincón = *l rinkōn* = एल रिन्कोन
48. Coward = El/La cobarde = *l kobaarde* = एल कोबारदे

49. Cow = La vaca = *laa baaka* = ला बाका
50. Crime = El delito = *l deylito* = एल देलीतो
51. Crop = El cultivo = *l cooltivo* = एल कुलतीवो
52. Crow = El cuervo = *l cooerbo* = एल कुएरवो
53. Crown = La corona = *laa koronaa* = ला कोरोना
54. Custody = La custodia = *laa koostodiya* = ला कूसतोदिया
55. Dance = El baile = *l bailey* = एल बाइले
56. Danger = El peligro = *l pēeliigro* = एल पेलिग्रो
57. Date = La fecha = *laa feechaa* = ला फेचा
58. Day = El día = *l diya* = एल दीया
59. Death = La muerte = *laa moaerte* = ला मूऐरते
60. Decoration = La decoración = *laa deecorasii-on* = ला देकोरासीओन
61. Deer = El venado = *l beenaado* = एल बेनादो
62. Department = El departamento = *l deepaartamento* = एल देपारतामेन्तो
63. Desert = El desierto = *l deciertō* = एल देसिएरतो
64. Dog = El perro = *l pērrro* = एल पेररो
65. Door = La puerta = *laa pooertaa* = ला पुएरता
66. Doubt = La duda = *laa dooda* = ला दूदा
67. Dozen = La docena = *laa dôcenaa* = ला दोसेना

68. Dream	=	El sueño	=	*l śûenyo*	=	एल सुएन्यो
69. Dress	=	El bebida	=	*l veestîdo*	=	एल बेसतिदो
70. Drink	=	La bedida	=	*laa beebîda*	=	ला! बेबिदा
71. Drop	=	La gota	=	*laa gôtaa*	=	ला गोता
72. Duck	=	El pato	=	*l paato*	=	एल पातो
73. Dump	=	El mudo	=	*l mûdoo*	=	एल मुदो
74. Dust	=	El polvo	=	*l pôlvoo*	=	एल पोलबो
75. Eagle	=	La águila	=	*laa â-guilaa*	=	ला आगीला
76. Ear	=	La oreja	=	*laa ôrējaa*	=	ला ओरेखा
77. Earth	=	La tierra	=	*laa tîerra*	=	ला तीएररा
78. East	=	El este	=	*l êste*	=	एल एस्ते
79. Echo	=	El eco	=	*l eko*	=	एल एको
80. Economy	=	La economía	=	*laa ekônomia*	=	ला एकोनोमिया
81. Editor	=	El editor	=	*L editôr*	=	एल एदीतोर
82. Education	=	La ensenanza	=	*laa ensenânzaa*	=	ला एनसेनानसा
83. Eclipse	=	El eclipse	=	*l eclîpse*	=	एल एकलीपसे
84. Elbow	=	El codo	=	*l cȯ̂do*	=	एल कोदो
85. End	=	El final	=	*l fînaal*	=	एल फीनाल

86. Energy	=	La energia	=	*enêrkhia*	=	ला एनेरखीआ
87. Environment	=	El ambiente	=	*âmbiente*	=	एल आमबिएनते
88. Event	=	El suceso	=	*l sûceso*	=	एल सुसेसो
89. Eye	=	El ojo	=	*l okho*	=	एल ओखो
90. Eye brow	=	La ceja	=	*Laa sekha*	=	ला सेखा
91. Eye lashes	=	Las pestañas	=	*Laas pêstanas*	=	लारा पेसतान्यास
92. Eye witness	=	El testigo	=	*l têstiigo*	=	एल तेसतीगो
93. Face	=	La cara	=	*Laa kara*	=	ला कारा
94. Fair	=	La feria	=	*Laa pheiira*	=	ला फेईरा
95. Fan	=	El abanico	=	*l âbanîico*	=	एल आबानिको
96. Farm	=	La hacienda	=	*Laa acianda*	=	ला आसीएनदा
97. Father	=	El padre	=	*l pâdre*	=	एल पाद्रे
98. Fire	=	El fuego	=	*l phuego*	=	एल फुएगो
99. Finger	=	El dedo	=	*l dedo*	=	एल देदो
100. Fish	=	La pez	=	*Laa pês*	=	ला पेस
101. Flag	=	La bandera	=	*laa baandêraa*	=	ला बानदेरा
102. Flame	=	La llama	=	*laa yama*	=	ला यामा
103. Flesh	=	La carne	=	*laa karne*	=	ला कारने
104. Fly	=	La mosca	=	*laa moosca*	=	ला मासका

105. Floor = El piso = *l piiso* = एल पीसो
106. Flour = La harina = *laa arinaa* = ला आरीना
107. Flower = La flor = *laa philôr* = ला फ्लोर
108. Flower pot = La maseta = *laa maaseta* = ला मासेता
109. Flute = La flauta = *laa phlaauta* = ला फलाऊता
110. Foam = La espuma = *laa aspûma* = ला एसपुमा
111. Fog = La niebla = *laa nûbla* = ला नीएबला
112. Foot = El pie = *l piee* = एल पीए
113. Forehead = La mente = *laa mente* = ला मेनते
114. Fort = la fortaleza = *laa phortalasa* = ला फोरतालेसा
115. Fountain = La fuente = *laa phuentee* = ला फुएनते
116. Frog = El/La gabacho/a = *l/laa gabaacho/a* = एल / ला गाबाचो / आ
117. Fuel = El combustible = *L komboosliiblay* = एल कोमबूस्तिइले
118. Function = La función = *laa phunciôn* = ला फुनसीओन
119. Future = El futuro = *l phuturo* = एल फुतुरो
120. Gamble = El riesgo = *l riesgoo* = एल रीएसगो
121. Garbage = La basura = *laa baasûra* = ला बासुरा
122. Garden = El járdin = *l khardin* = एल खारदीन

123. Girl = La chica = *La chica* = ला चीका
124. Glass = El cristal/El vaso = *l kristal* = एल क्रीसताल
125. Glove = La guante = *Laa guaante* = ला गुआनते
126. Glue = El pegamento = *l pagamanto* = एल पेगामेनतो
127. Goat = La cabra = *la kabra* = ला काबरा
128. God = El dios = *l diôs* = एल दीओस
129. Gold = El oro = *l orô* = एल ओरो
130. Grand father = El abuelo = *l âbueloo* = एल आबुएलो
131. Grand mother = La abuela = *l âbuelaa* = ला आबुएला
132. Grape = La uva = *Laa uvaa* = ला ऊबा
133. Grave = La sepultura = *Laa Sapultûraa* = ला सेपुलतुरा
134. Guard = el guardía = *L gooardiaa* = एल गुआरदिया
135. Guest = El invitado = *inbîtadoo* = एल इनबितादो
136. Gum = La goma = *laa gômaa* = ला गोमा
137. Habit = El hábito = *l abitoo* = एल आबितो
138. Hair = El pelo = *l pêlo* = एल पेलो
140. Hand = La mano = *Laa manoo* = ला मानो
141. Hammer = El martillo = *l mârtiyo* = एल मारतीयो

142. Hazard = El peligro = *l peeligroo* = स पेलीग्रो
143. Head = La mente = *Laa meente* = ला मेनते
144. Heap = El menton = *l mentôn* = एल मेनतोन
145. Heart = El corazón = *l korasôn* = एल कोरासोन
146. Heat = El Calor = *l kalor* = एल कालोर
147. Heel = El talón = *l taalôn* = एल तालोन
148. Hip = La cadera = *Laa kadera* = ला कादेरा
149. History = La histioria = *Laa istoria* = ला इसतोरिया
150. Hole = El agjero = *l agkheroo* = एल आगखेरो
151. Home = La casa = *Laa caasa* = ला कासा
152. Honey = La miel = *Laa miêl* = ला मिएल
153. Horn = El cuerno = *l ceûrno* = एल कुएरनो
154. Horse = El cabello = *l cabeyo* = एल काबेलो
155. Hour = La hora = *Laa ora* = ला ओरा
156. Husband = El esposo = *l espooso* = एल एसपोसो
157. Hypnosis = La hipnosis = *Laa ipnosis* = ला इपनोसिस
158. Importance = La importancia = *Laa importancia* = ला इमपोरतानसिया
159. Industrial = Industrial = *Laa indûstrîaal* = ला इन्दुसत्रिआल

160. Information	=	La infromacion	=	*Laa informaâcîon*	=	ला इनफोर. मासिओन
161. Jewellery	=	La joya	=	*laa khoya*	=	ला खोया
162. Joke	=	El chiste	=	*l chistee*	=	एल चीसते
163. Judgment	=	La sentencia	=	*Laa sentencia*	=	ला सेनतेनसीआ
164. Key	=	La llave	=	*Laa yavee*	=	ला याबे
165. Knife	=	El cuchillo	=	*l cuchiyo*	=	एल कुचीयो
166. Knot	=	El nudo	=	*l nōodo*	=	एल नुदो
167. Knee	=	La rodilla	=	*laa rodiya*	=	ला रोदीया
168. Knowledge	=	La sabiduría	=	*Laa sâbiaduriia*	=	ला साबिदुरीया
169. Laboratory	=	El laboratoria	=	*l labôratoriaa*	=	एल लाबोरातोरिया
170. Lad	=	El muchacho	=	*l muchaachoo*	=	एल मुचाचो
171. Lady	=	La mujer	=	*Laa mukher*	=	ला मुखेर
172. Lamb	=	El cordero	=	*l cordero*	=	ला कोरदेरो
173. Land	=	La tierra	=	*Laa tiêrra*	=	ला तीएररा
174. Lane	=	El camino	=	*l kamino*	=	एल कामीनो
175. Language	=	La lengua	=	*Laa lenguāa*	=	ला लेनगुआ
176. Lap	=	El regazo	=	*l rêgaso*	=	एल रेगासो
177. Laughter	=	La risa	=	*Laa risāa*	=	ला रीसा
178. Law	=	La ley	=	*Laa lei*	=	ला लेई

179. Leaf = La hoja = *Laa okha* = ला ओखा
180. Leather = El cuero = *l kuero* = एल कुएरो
181. Leopard = El leopardo = *l leopaardo* = एल लेओपारदो
182. Lemon = El limón = *l limoon* = एल लिमोन
183. Lettuce = La lechuga = *Laa lechôogaa* = ला लेचुगा
184. Life = La vida = *Laa bida* = ला बिदा
185. Leg = La pie = *Laa piie* = ला पाए
186. Lip = El labio = *l laabio* = एल लाबियो
187. Literature = La literatura = *Laa litaraturaa* = ला लितेरातुरा
188. Lock = La cerradura = *Laa ceîraduraa* = ला सेररादुरा
189. Lotus = El loto = *l loto* = एल लोतो
190. Love = El amor = *l amoor* = एल आमोर
191. Lover = El amante = *l aamantē* = एल आमानते
192. Lunch = El almuerzo = *l almuersoo* = एल अलमुएरसो
193. Lung = El pulmón = *l pûlmôon* = एल पुलमोन
194. Magic = La magia = *Laa makhia* = ला माखीआ
195. Magnet = El imán = *l imaan* = एल इमान
196. Maid = La criada = *Laa kriada* = ला क्रीआदा

197.	Majority	=	La mayoría	=	*Laa mayoriia*	=	ला मायोरिया
198.	Man	=	El hombre	=	*l Ombre*	=	एल ओम्ब्रे
199.	Map	=	El mapa		*l Mapāa*	=	एल मापा
200.	Massage	=	El mensaje	=	*l mensaakhe*	=	एल मान्साखे
201.	Material	=	La materia	=	*Laa materiia*	=	ला मातेरिया
202.	Meal	=	La comida	=	*Laa comida*	=	ला कोमिदा
203.	Medicine	=	La medicina	=	*Laa mediciina*	=	ला मेदिसीना
204.	Melon	=	El melón	=	*l miloon*	=	एल मेलोन
205.	Mind	=	La mente	=	*Laa mente*	=	ला मेनते
206.	Mirror	=	El espejo	=	*l aspekho*	=	एल एसपेखो
207.	Monument	=	El monumento	=	*l monōomento*	=	एल मोनुमेनतो
208.	Mosquito	=	El mosquito	=	*l moskito*	=	एल मोसकीतो
209.	Murder	=	El acesinado	=	*l acesinaado*	=	एल आसेसीनादो
210.	Mustache	=	El bigote	=	*l biigôte*	=	एल बिगोते
211.	Mustard	=	La mostaza	=	*Laa mostasaa*	=	ला मोसतासा
212.	Mystery	=	El misterio	=	*l misteerio*	=	एल मिसतेरीयो
213.	Name	=	El nombre	=	*l nombree*	=	एल नामबरे
214.	Nationality	=	La nacionalidad	=	*Laa naciônalidaad*	=	ला नासिओनालिदाद
215.	Nature	=	La naturaleza	=	*Laa naturaatesa*	=	ला नुतुरालेसा

	English		Spanish		Pronunciation		Hindi
216.	Need	=	La necesidad	=	*Laa necesidaad*	=	ला नेसेसीदाद
217.	Needle	=	La aguja	=	*Laa agukha*	=	ला आगुखा
218.	Neighbour	=	El vecino	=	*l becino*	=	एल बेसीनो
219.	Nest	=	El nido	=	*l nido*	=	एल निदो
220.	News	=	La noticia	=	*Laa noticiia*	=	ला नोतिसीआ
221.	Night	=	La noche	=	*Laa nochê*	=	ला नोचे
222.	Nose	=	La náriz	=	*Laa naaris*	=	ला नारीस
223.	Neck	=	El cuello	=	*l cueyo*	=	एल कुयेओ
224.	Nail	=	La uña	=	*Laa unya*	=	ला उन्या
225.	Onion	=	La cebolla	=	*Laa ceboya*	=	ला सेबोया
226.	Owl	=	La lechuza	=	*Laa lechusa*	=	ला लेचुसा
227.	Pain	=	El dolor	=	*l doloor*	=	एल दोलोर
228.	Palm	=	La palma	=	*Laa palmaa*	=	ला पालमा
229.	Parrot	=	El loro	=	*l loroo*	=	एल लोरो
230.	Patient	=	La/El paciente	=	*laa/l pacientee*	=	ला/एल पासीएनते
231.	Peacock	=	El pavo	=	*l paavo*	=	एल पाबो
232.	People	=	La gente	=	*laa khente*	=	ला खेनते
233.	Pepper	=	La pimienta	=	*Laa pimientaa*	=	ला पीमीएनता

234. Person	=	El persona	=	*l personaa*	=	एल पेरसोना
235. Pillow	=	La almohada	=	*laa almoada*	=	ला आलमोआदा
236. Place	=	El lugar	=	*l lugaar*	=	एल लुगार
237. Poison	=	El veneno	=	*l venenoo*	=	एल बेनेनो
238. Population	=	La poblacio'n	=	*Laa pablacioon*	=	ला पोबलासियोन
239. Pot	=	El tarrop	=	*l tarrop*	=	एल ताररोप
240. Potato	=	La patata	=	*Laa pataata*	=	ला पाताता
241. Prayer	=	El rezo	=	*l reso*	=	एल रेसो
242. Price	=	El precio	=	*l precioo*	=	एल प्रेसीओ
243. Prize	=	El premio	=	*l premiio*	=	एल प्रेमीओ
244. Prince	=	El principe	=	*l principe*	=	एल प्रीनसीपे
245. Princess	=	La princesa	=	*Laa princesaa*	=	ला प्रीनसेसा
246. Queen	=	La reina	=	*Laa reinaa*	=	ला रेईना
247. Question	=	La cuestión	=	*laa kuestion*	=	ला कुएसतीओन
248. Rabbit	=	El/La conejo/a	=	*l/laa conekho/a*	=	एल/ला कोनेखो
249. Race	=	La carrera	=	*Laa carrera*	=	ला काररेरा
250. Reáson	=	La razón	=	*laa rason*	=	ला रासोन
251. Refugee	=	El refugido	=	*l rephukhido*	=	एल रेफुखीदो
252. Residence	=	La residensia	=	*Laa residenciaa*	=	ला रेसीदेनसीआ

253. River	=	El río	=	*l riô*	=	एल रीओ
254. Rock	=	La roca	=	*l rooca*	=	ला रोका
255. Roof	=	El techo	=	*l teecho*	=	एल तेचो
256. Root	=	El raíz	=	*l raais*	=	एल राईस
257. Rose	=	La rosa	=	*Laa rosaa*	=	ला रोसा
258. Sacred	=	Sagrado	=	*saagrado*	=	साग्रादो
259. Salary	=	El sueldo	=	*l sûeldo*	=	एल सुएलदो
260. Salt	=	La sal	=	*Laa saal*	=	ला साल
261. Sand	=	La arena	=	*Laa arenaa*	=	ला आरेना
262. Scorpion	=	El escorpóin	=	*l escorpooin*	=	एल एसकोरपोईन
263. Season	=	La estacion	=	*Laa estacion*	=	ला एसतासिओन
264. She	=	Ella	=	*El-ya*	=	एया / एल्या
265. Sheet	=	La sabana	=	*laa sabaana*	=	ला साबाना
266. Song	=	La canción	=	*Laa canciôn*	=	ला कानसीओन
267. Skin	=	La piel	=	*Laa piêl*	=	ला पीएल
268. Sky	=	El cielo	=	*l ciêlo*	=	एल सिएलो
269. Slap	=	La palmada	=	*Laa palmaada*	=	ला पालमादा
270. Snake	=	El serpiente	=	*l sêrpîente*	=	एल सेरपीएनते

271. Society = La sociedad = *Laa sociedaad* = ला सोसिएदाद
272. South = La sur = *Laa sûr* = ला सुर
273. Spoon = La cuchara = *Laa cuchara* = ला कुचारा
274. Thing = La cosa = *Laa cosa* = ला कोसा
275. Thigh = El muslo = *l mûslo* = एल मुसलो
276. Thousand = El mil = *l mil* = एल मील
277. Time = El tiempo = *l tiêmpo* = एल तीएमपो
278. Toe = El dedo = *dêdo* = एल देदो
278. Tooth = El diente = *l diênti* = एल दीएन्ते
280. Trade = El negocio = *l negocio* = एल नेगोसीओ
281. Ultimatum = El ultimatúm = *l ultimatûm* = एल ऊलतीमातुम
282. Umbrella = El paragua = *l paragûa* = एल पारागुआ
283. Vegetable = El legumbre = *l legûmbre* = एल लेगुमब्रे
284. Vehicle = El vehículo = *veîculo* = एल बेईकुलो
285. Village = El pueblo = *l puêbloo* = एल पुएबलो
286. Violet = La violeta = *laa vii-oletaa* = ला वियोलेता

287. Waist = La cintura = *Laa ciïntūraa* = ला सीनतुरा
288. Water = El agua = *l âgua* = एल आगुआ

289. Wave = La ola = *Laa ôla* = ला ओला
290. Wax = La cera = *Laa cêra* = ला सेरा
291. Weapon = La arma = *Laa ârma·* = ला आरमा
292. Week = La semana = *laa semana* = ला सेमाना
293. Weight = El peso = *l pêso* = एल पेसो
294. West = El oeste = *l ôeste* = एल ओएस्ते
295. Wheel = La rueda = *Laa ruêda* = ला रूएदा
296. Wind = El viente = *l viênte* = एल बिएनते
297. Woman = La mujer = *Laa mukher* = ला मुखेर
298. Word = La palabra = *Laa pâlabra* = ला पालाब्रो
299. Work = El trabajo = *l trabakho* = एल त्राबाखो
300. World = El mundo = *l mûndo* = एल मुनदो
301. Worship = La adoración = *laa aado-rasion* = ला अदोरासीओन
302. Year = El año = *l anyo* = एल आन्यो
303. Yesterday = Ayer = *âyer* = आयेर
304. Youth = La mocedad = *Laa môcedaad* = ला मोसेदाद

Introduce yourself

1. I am British
   Soy un británico
   Soi ûn Britaanicô
   सोई उन ब्रीतानिको!
2. But I have US citizenship
   Pero, tengo ciudadaína Americana.
   Pēerō tēengo siiudādaniya aamēiriikana
   पेरो तेंगो सिऊदादानिया आमेरिकाना।
3. I have come from Singapore
   Soy de singapur.
   Soi dēe siingāapoor.
   सोई दे सिंगापूर।
4. Oh, my name is ....
   Oye, me llamo...........
   Oii-yē mēe layāamo
   ओइए में लयामों

5. I am a teacher by profession.
   Soy un maestro de profesión
   Soi ûn māaēstro dēe prōfēesiion
   सोई ऊन माइस्त्रो दे प्रोफेसियोन।
6. My hobbies are-travelling and writing
   Mis pasatiempos son viajar y escribir

Miss pāasātiiēmpōs sō-on viiahāar e ēskriibiir
मिस पासातियमपोस सोन वियाखार ई एसीक्रिबिर।

7. I have a passport valid upto ....
Tengo un pasaporate válido hasta
Tēengo un pāasāportē vāalidō astaa ....
तेंगों उन पासपोरते बालिदों आस्ता ....

8. My visa Lasts on ....
Mi visa termina el
Me viisāa tēeraniina l
मि वीसा तेरमिना एल ....

9. I am married.
Estoy casado.
Ēstoi kasāado.
एसतोई कसादों।

10. No, my wife has not come with me.
No, mi esposa no ha venido conmigo.
No me ēspōsāa no āa vēeniidō konmiigo.
नों मी एसपोसा नो आ वेनिदों कोनामिगों।

11. I have come alone.
He venido sólo.
A vēniidō sō-lō.
ए वेनिदों सोलो।

12. I have never been to this country before.
No he estado antes en este páis.
No a ēstāadō aantēs ēen ēestēe pāaiis.
नो ए एसतादो आनतेस एन एस्ते पाइस।

13. Along with MountAbu, I have to visit Jaipur also.

Junto con Mountabu, tambien que visitar a jaipur.

Khoontō kon mount AABU tāambiiēen K biisiitāar āa Jaipur.

खुनतो कोन माऊट आबु ताम्बिएन के बिसितार आ जयपुर।

14. I'll catch my flight back on ....

Voy a coger el avión de vuelto.

Voiî aa kōkhēer l day booēelto.

वोई आ कोसेर एल आबियोन दे बुप्लतो।

15. My height is 6ft. 2inches.

Mido 6 pies 2 pulgadas.

Miidō sēeiis pee-s dōs poolgāadas.

मिदो सेईस पिएस दोस पुलगादास।

16. My weight is 82 kilograms.

Peso 82 kgs

pēesō ochtentāa e dōs kiilogrāamāmāas.

पेसो आचेतेन्ता इ दोस 82 किलोग्रामास।

17. I have got my suite booked at hotel Radisson.

Tengo una suite reservada en el hotel Radission.

Tēengo unāa suite rēesērvāada n l otēel rēdiîsōn.

तेगों उना सुईट रेसेरवादा एन एल ओतेल रांदिसन।

18. I have visited almost the whole of Europe.

He visitado casí toda Europa.

A Bzeetāadō kāāsiî tōdāa aoorōpāa

ए बिजितादो कासी तोदा एउरोपा।

19. I find hospitality of Indians really great.

Me parace la hospitalidad de los indios muy buena.

Mēe pāarēse laa ospiitāaliiāad dēe lōs indii-os mooii booēenō

मे पारेसे ला ओसपितालिदाद दे लोस इंदियोस मुई बुयेना।

20. I prefer vegetarian food.
Prefiero la comida vegetariana.
prey-fii-ēro laa Komiidāa Bēekhēetāariî-āana.
प्रफियेरो ला कोमिदा भेखेखारियाना।

21. I have a good camera.
Tengo una cámara buena.
Tēengo oonā kamara booena.
तेंगो उना कामारा बुयना।

22. My luggage is light and simple.
Mi equipaje es ligero y sencillo.
Me A-ki-pāa-khe ēes liikhēerō e sēensiiyo.
मि एकिपारवे एस लिरवेरो ईसियों।

23. I have not brought my laptop computer.
No he traido mi laptop.
No A trāaiidō me laptop.
नो ए त्राइदो मी लापतोप।

24. I will take some books with me.
Tomaré algunos libros conmigo.
Tōmāarey aalgoonos liibrōs kōmiigo.
तोमारे आलगुनोस लिबरोस कोन मिगो।

25. I can give you this book free.
Puedo darte este libro por gratis.

Pooedō dāartēe A-stay lee-brō : pōr grāatiis.
पुएदो दारते एसते लिबरो पोर ग्रातिस।

At the customs

1. Do I have to fill up any papers?
?Tengo que rellenar algunos papeles?
Tēengo K Ray-len-yaar aalgoon-os pāapēeless ?
टं तेगों के रेलेनार आलगुनोस पापेलेस?
2. Where do I sign?
?Dónde firmo?
Dōn-dēe fiirmō
दोंदे फिरमो ?
3. Yes, both these black bags are mine!
Sí, estas ambas bolsas negras son mías.
see A-Staes aambass bolsāas naygrass sōn miiaas.
सि एसतास आम्बास बोलसास नेगरास सोन मियास ?
4. No, that leather suitcase is not mine.
No, esa maleta de cuero no es mía.
No A-sāa māaletāa day kooerō no ēes miiyā ?
नो एसा मालेता दे कुएरो ना एस मिया ?
5. What do I have to declare?
?Qué tengo que declarar?
K tēengo K Day-Klāa-rāar
के तेगों के देकेलारार ?
6. Is this bottle of perfume dutiable?

Es esta botella de perfume sujeta a derechos de aduana?

A-s A-stā Bōtēeyāa dēe pēerfoomēe sukhetāa āa dērechoos dēe aadooana ?

एस एसता बोतेएया दे पेराफुमे सुखेता आ देरेचोस दे आदुआना ?

7. Can I import this bottle of wine?

Puedo importar esta botella de cerveza?

pooedō im-pōr-taar A-stāa Botēeya dēe Serbēesa.

पुयेदों एम्पोरतार एस्ता बोतोया दे सेरबेसा ?

8. Yes, this is my health certificate.

Sí, este es mi certificado de salud.

See, A-stay As me sērtiifiikāadō day mii sāalood.

सि एस्ते एस मि सेरतिफिकादो दे मि सालुद।

9. These are my personal belongings?

Estos son mis efectos personales.

A-Stōs sōn miss A-fek-tōs pēer-so-nāales.

एस्तोस सोन मिस ऐफेक्तोस पेरसोनालेस।

10. Do I have to open the bag?

Tengo que abrir la bolsa?

Tēengo K aabriîr laa Bōlsāa ?

तेंगों के आ़बरिर ला बोलसा ?

11. Where is the toilet?

?Dónde está el servicio?

Dōnday A-Stāa l sēervii-see-o.

दोन्दे एस्ता एल सेरविसियो.

12. Is there a coffee shop here?
Hay una cafetería por aquí?
Āaii oonāa kofētēria pōr āakii?
आई उना काफेतेरिया पोर आकी ?

13. How can I reach hotel Radission?
Cómo se puede llegar al hotel Radisson?
Kōmo say pooedayegāar l otēel Radiison.
कोमो से पुएदे ल्यागार आल ओतेल रैडिसन

14. How far it is?
Cuánto lejos está?
Kooantōs lēekhōs A-stāa ?
कुआन्तोस लेखोस एस्ता ?

15. Where can I get a taxi?
Dónde puedo coger un taxi?
Dōn-day pooedō kokhēr oon Taxi ?
दोन्दे पुएदो कोखेर उन ताक्सी ?

16. Can I get Indian currency here?
Puedo consequir la moneda de la India aquí?
Pooedō kōnsēegiir laa mōnēedā day laa iindiiāa aaki ?
पुएदो कोन्सेगिर ला मोनेदो दे ला इंदिया आकि ?

17. Do you have traveler's cheques?
Tienes cheques de viajeros?
Tee-a-ness chēe-kess day biakheros?
तिएनेस चेकेस दे बियाखेरोस?

18. Kindly give me the receipt.
Tenga la bondad de darme la receta.

Tēenga laa bōndāad day dāar mēe laa ray-say-tāa.

तेंगो ला बोनदाद दे दार मे ला रेसेता।

19. How about these US made medicines?

Qué piensas sobre las medicinas fabricadas en los Estados Unidos?

K pee-n-saas so-bray laas mēe diisināas faabriiKaados n lōs A-stāadōs ooniidōs.

के पिएसास सोबरे लास मेडिसीनास फाबरिकादास एन लोस एस्तादोस उनिदोस?

20. They are for my personal use

Son para mi Uso personal.

Sōn pāara me ooso pēer-so-naal.

सोन पारा मि उसो पेरसोनाल।

21. Thank god, that I can carry them.

Gracias a dios, que puedo llevarlos.

Graasiaas aa Diī-os K pooedō yēevāarlos.

ग्रासियास आ दिओस के पुयोदो लेवार लोस।

22. Well, kindly guide me to the exit.

Pues, tenga la bondad de dirigirme a la salida.

pooēs tēengāa laa bone-dāad day diîriî. Khir mēe aa laa sāaliîda.

पुयेस तेंगा ला बोनदाद, दे दिरीखिर में आ ला सालिदा।

23. Do you speak english?

Hablas inglés?

aablāas eeng-less?

आबलास इन्गलेस ?

24. Kindly explain my problem to the taxi driver.

Tenga la bondad de expelicarle al conductor mi problema.

Tēengāa laa bone-dāad day x-pliikāarlēe all kōndooktōr me problay-māa.

तेंगा ला बोनदाद दे एक्सपिलाकार ले आल कोन्दुक्तोर मि प्रोबलेमा।

25. Is there a bus or train service to the city?

Hay un servicio de autobús o ferrocaril a la ciudad?

I oon sēer-b-c-o day aaootōboos o fero-ka-ril, aa laa see-u-dāad ?

आई उन सेरबिसियो दे आउतोबुस ओ फेरोकारिल आ ला सिउदाद?

Conversation with the taxi driver

1. Can you take me to hotel Radisson
?Puedes llevarme al hotel Radisson?
Pooedēes levāar-mēe āa otēel Radisson ?
पुऐदेस लेवारमें आ ओतेल रेडिसन ?
2. Yes, I have got a booking there.
Sí, tengo una reserva allí.
See tēengo ray-servāa aaliî.
सि तेंगों रेसेरबा आलि।
3. How much will you charge?
cúantos cobbras?
Kwāantōs kōbrāas?
क्वान्तोस कोबरास?
4. Three hundred rupees are too much.
Es demasiado 300 rupias.
A-s day-māasiiadō dōs-seeyentāas roopyaas.
एस देमासीयादो दोससियलास रूपयास।
5. I have seen the rate list.
He visto la lista de precio.
A Beestō laa lee-stāa day Prey-sii-yos.
ए बिस्तो ला लिस्ता दे प्रेसियोस।
6. Two hundred rupees are enough.
Es bastante 200 rupias.

Conversation with the taxi driver

1. Can you take me to hotel Radisson
   ?Puedes llevarme al hotel Radisson?
   Pooedēes levāar-mēe āa otēel Radisson ?
   पुऐदेस लेवारमें आ ओतेल रेडिसन ?
2. Yes, I have got a booking there.
   Sí, tengo una reserva allí.
   See tēengo ray-servāa aaliî.
   सि तेंगों रेसेरबा आलि।
3. How much will you charge?
   cúantos cobbras?
   Kwāantōs kōbrāas?
   क्वान्तोस कोबरास?
4. Three hundred rupees are too much.
   Es demasiado 300 rupias.
   A-s day-māasiiadō dōs-seeyentāas roopyaas.
   एस देमासीयादो दोससियलास रूपयास।
5. I have seen the rate list.
   He visto la lista de precio.
   A Beestō laa lee-stāa day Prey-sii-yos.
   ए बिस्तो ला लिस्ता दे प्रेसियोस।
6. Two hundred rupees are enough.
   Es bastante 200 rupias.

A-s Baanstaantēe dō-see-n-tāas

एस बास्तांते दो सियेंतास रूपयास

7. O.K., you load this luggage.

Vale, carga este equipaje.

Baale Karga A-stay a-ki-pa-khe.

बाले कारगा ऐस्ते एकिपाखे।

8. How long will it take to reach?

Cuánto tarda llegar allí?

Kwantō tāardā llegaar aali.

क्वान्तो तारदा लियेगार आली ?

9. Since when you are driving in this city?

Hace cuándo conduces en esta ciudad?

asēe cooandō kōndoosēes ēen ěestaa seeoodāad?

आसे कुआंदों कोन्दुसेस एन एस्ता सिउदाद।

10. Can I hire your taxi for a full day?

Puedo alquilar tu taxi para un día entero?

Pooedō aalkiilaar tōo tāaksii paara oon diya n-tēe-ro ?

पुएदो आलकीलार तु ताक्सी पारा उन दिया एनतेरो?

11. Will you charge on hourly basis?

Cobras por hora?

kōbrās pōr orāa ?

कोबरास पोर ओरा ?

12. Or according to distace?.

O por distancia?

O pōr orāa ?

ओ पोर दिस्तानसिया ?

13. How can I contact you?
Cómo puedo contactarte?
Kōmo pooedō kōntaktāar-te ?
कोमो पुऐदो कोन्ताक्तारते ?

14. Well, we are almost there.
Pues casí estamos allí.
pooēes kāasi A-staamos aalii.
पुऐस कासी एसतामोस आली।

15. Thank you for this interesting ride.
Gracias para esta vuelta interesante.
Graasiiās pāara A-stāa Booeltāa in-tērēe-sāan-te.
ग्रारसिआस पारा एस्ता बुएलता इन्तेरेसान्ते।

At the hotel

1. I hope I have got a reservation.
   Espero que tenga yo reserva.
   espero ke tenga yô reservaa.
   एसपेरो के तेनगा यो रेसेरबा।
2. Yes, I asked for a single bed room
   Sí, pedí una habitación individual.
   Si Peđî ûna abitaciôn individuâl.
   सी पेदी ऊना आबितासिओन इनदिबिदुआल।
3. I had wired from Singapore.
   Mandéun telegrama de Singapur.
   Mandé ûn telegramaa da Singapûr.
   मानदे ऊन तेलेग्रामा दे सिंगापुर।
4. I sent it about a week ago.
   Lo envié hace casí una semana.
   Lû envíe ace casî ûna sēmāna.
   लो एनबीए आसे कासी ऊना समाना।
5. Oh, thank god that I have got my room.
   Oye gracias a dios que he conseguido mi habitación.
   Oye, Gracias a diôs ke consaguidôo mî abitation.
   ओई ग्रासिआस अ दिओस के ए कोनसेगीदो मी आबीतसिओन।
6. No, I failed to wire you in advance.

No, fracase escribirte en avanze.
No, frāakaasay s-kriibiirtay n avaantey
नो, फ्राकासे एसक्रीबीरते एन अबानसे।

7. Kindly, try your best.
Tenga la bondad de tratar cuanto puedas.
Tengâ la Bondaad de Trâtaar Kuanto pooedāas.
तेंगा ला बोनदाद दे त्रातार कुआन्तो पुएदास।

8. O.K., a double bed room will do.
Vale, habitación doble está bien.
bale abitaciôn dobla astâ bien.
वाले, आबितासिओन दोबले एस्ता बीएन।

9. How much will it be?
cuánto cuesta?
Kooantō Kuesta ?
कुआन्तो कुएसता ?

10. Quite reasonable.
Muy razonable.
Mui rasonable :
मुई रासोनाबले।

11. Oh, it's quite expensive.
Oye , es muy caro.
Oye, as mui caro.
ओईए, एस मुई कारो।

12. Does it include any meals?
Incluye las comidas?
enclûe laas conidaas ?
इनक्लूए लास कोमिदास ?

13. I have to stay for three days.

Tengo que quedar para tres días.
Tengo ke kedar pâra três diâs.
तेंगो के केदार पारा त्रेस दिआस।

14. No, for one night only.
No, solamente para una noche.
No, solamênte pâra Ûna noche.
नो, सोलामेनते पारा ऊना नोचे।

15. It is quite small.
Es muy pequeño.
as mui pekenyo
एस मुई पेकेन्यो

16. It is not cool.
No es frío.
No, as frîo.
नो, एस फ्रिओ।

17. The window does not face the sea.
La ventana no da al mar.
Laa Bentana no da all maar.
ला बेनताना नो दा आल मार।

18. It doesn't appear adequately clean.
No parece limpio propiamente.
No, parēce limpîo propîamente.
नो, पारेसे लीमपीओ प्रोपियामेनते।

19. Kindly clean it first.
Porfavor, limpialo primero.
Por phabor, limpîalo, primero.
पोर फाबोर, लिमपीआलो, प्रीमेरो।

20. How can I get some fresh air?

Cómo puedo tomar el aire fresco?
Cômo pooedo Tomaar l aîre phresco.
कोमो पुएदो तोमार एल आइरे प्रेसको ?

21. Do you have air conditioned rooms?
Tienes habitaciones aire condiconadas?
Tiênes tras abitaciônes aîre acondiciôn-asas.
तीएनेस त्रेस आबितासिओनेस आईरे आकोनदि–सीयोनादोस ?

22. What will be the extra charge?
Oué será el precio extra?
Ke Serâ l precio extra ?
के सेरा एल प्रेसीओ एक्सत्रा ?

23. Can I check out at 10.00AM?
Puedo dejar el hotel a las diez?
Puêdo dekhar âl otai āa laas đies.
पुएदो देखार एल ओतेल आ आलास दिएस ?

24. Is credit card facility available?
Está disponible la tarjeta del credíto?
astâ disponîblē laa tarkheta dél krādîto ?
एसता दिसपोनिबले ला तारखेता देल क्रेदीतो ?

25. Does the bank have ATM facility?
Teine el banco la facilidad de cajero automatico?
Tiêne el banko laa facilidad da cakhêro automâtico.
तिएने एल बांको ला फासिलिदाद दे कारवेरो अऊतोमातिको ?

26. Where is my key?

Dónde está mi llave?
Dôndē estâ mî yabe ?
दोन्दे एसता मी ल्याबे ?

27. Here is my key.
Aquí está mi llave.
Âki astâ mî yabe.
आकी एसता मी ल्याबे।

28. No, I am a vegetarian.
No,Soy vegetariano.
Soi, Vekhétarîano.
सोइ, बेखेतारीआनो।

29. I eat eggs.
Como huevos.
Como uabos.
कोमो उएबोस।

30. Can I order wine in my room?
Puedo pedir vino en mi cuarto?
Pûedo pedîr Vîno an mî Kuartoo ?
पुएदो पेदीर बीनो इन मी कुआरतो ?

31. Am I allowed to take my lady friends to my room?
?Se permite llevar mis amigas al cuarto?
Sa permite yabaar mîs āamigo al kuartoo ?
से पेरमीते ल्येवार मीस आमीगो आल कुअरतो ?

32. What are the means of entertainment available here?
Cuáles son los medios de entretenimiento disponible aquí?

Kualás sôn lôs meďios da entretenimîento disponîble akî ?
कुओलेस सोन लोस मेदीओस दे एनत्रेतेनीमीइनतो दिसपोनीबले आकी ?

33. Hello reception! Kindly connect me to phone number........!
Hola recepción porfavor pongame el contácto con el numeró de teléfono.
Ola recepeûn, Por phabor, pôngame contâcto côn el nûmero de telephono.
ओला रेसेपसिओन, पोर फाबोर पोंगामे एल कोनताकतो कोन एल नुमेरो दे तेलेफोनो।

34. Send him/her up to my room.
Dirigele el/ella arriba a mi cuarto.
Dirikhele al/alla arriba āa mî kuarto.
दिरिखेले एल/एल्या आररीबा आ मी कुआरतो।

35. Tell him/her to wait in the lobby.
Dile a el/ella que me espere en vestibulo.
Dile āa al/alla ke ma aspare en vestibûlo.
दीले आ एल/एल्या के में एसपेरे एन बेसतिबुलो।

36. I'll be there within half an hour.
Estaré allídentro de media hora.
astarê allî dêntro da meďia ora.
एसतारे आल्या देनत्रो दे मेदिया ओरा।

37. I will return in the evening.
Volvere por la tarde.
Volverê pôr laa taarde.
वोलबेरे पोर ला तारदे।

38. Tell the visitor to come on Monday.

Dígale al visitante que venga el lunes.
Dîle ke aal visitante ke Vênga l lûnes.
दिगा ले आलविसितांते के मेगा एल लुनेस।

39. It is room number three or four.
Es el cuarto numero tres cero cuatro.
as el kuarto nûmero toos sero kuatro.
एस एल कुआरतो नुमेरों त्रेस सेरो कुआतरो।

40. Send me some warm water.
Enviame un poquito agua caliente.
N-v-āạ-ney Ûn pôkito āagua cāliente.
उन पोकितो आगुआ कालियन्ते एनवियामे

41. By what time the lunch will be ready?
Hasta que hora el almuerzo estará preparado?
āsta ke ora l almûarso astarâ preparâdo.
आस्ता के ओरा एल आलमुएरसो एसतारा प्रेपारादो ?

42. Uptil what time you are open for the dinner?
?Hasta que está abierto para la cena?
āsta ke astâ abîerta para laa cena.
आस्ता के एसता आबिएरतो पारा ला सेना ?

43. What is the dish of the day?
Cuál es el plato del dia?
kual as l platoo dāl dīa ?
कुआल एस एल पलातो देल दिआ ?

44. Kindly serve the meal in my room!
Tenga la bondad de servirme la comida en mi cuarto.
Tánga laa bondaad dā servîr laa cômida en mî kuartoo.

तेंगो ला बोनदाद दे सेरबीर ला कोमिदा एन मी कुआरतो।

45. I am checking out.
    Voy a dejar el hotel.
    Voi ā dēkhār l otal.
    बोई आ देखार एल ओतेल।

46. Call a taxi for me.
    Traigame un taxi para.
    Traagame ûn tâxi parā mî.
    त्रइगामे ऊन तक्सी पारा मी।

47. Yes, straight to the Airport.
    Sí directamente al airopuerto.
    Sî diractamente aal airopûerṭo.
    सी, दिरेक्तामेन्ते आल आईरोपुएरतो।

At a tourist place

1. Is there any office of tourism department here?
   Hay una oficina de departamento turismo?
   I oonā o-fii-c-nāa day de-pāar-tāa-men-tō day tū-riis-mā ?
   आई उना ओफिसीना दे देपारतामेन्तो दे तूरिस्मो ?
2. Yes, I want a tourist guide.
   Si, necesito un guía
   see, nēe-sēe-sii-tō oon giiyāa
   सी, नेसेसितो उन गीया।
3. Are you a registered guide?
   ?Erés un guía registrado?
   A-ress oon giiya ray-khis-trāa-dō ?
   ए रेस उन गीया रेखिसत्रादो ?
4. Kindly show me your I-card.
   Tenga la bondad de mostrarme tu carnet.
   tēe-nga lāa bone-dāad day mās-traar-mēe tū kar-nayet.
   तेन्गा ला बोनदाद दे मोस्तरारमें तू कारनेत।
5. How much time will it take to see this place completely?
   Cuánto tarda ver este lugar completamente?
   Kuânto tâarda bayr-stay lûgar komplātāmānte ?
   कुआन्तो तारदा वेर एस्ते लुगामू कोम्पलेतामेन्ते ?

6. I do not have seven days..........will three days do?
No, tengo siete días ? bastarán tres días?
no tango sîate dí-as ? Baastarân trēess días ?
नो तेन्गो सीएते दियास वास्तारान त्रेस दियास ?
7. Do you charge your fee on daily basis?
Cobras por día?
kobras pôr dîa ?
कोबरास पोर दिया ?
8. How much do you charge for your package of three days?
Cuánto cobras para tres días en total?
kuânto kobras parâ tras dí-as an totâl ?
कुआन्तो कोब्रास पारा त्रेस दियास एन तोताल
9. Ok, get tickets for the three of us.
Vale, saca billetes para tres de nosotros.
baalay, saka biyetēs para tres daynosotrûs.
वाले साका वियेतेस पारा त्रेस दे नोसोत्रास।
10. Do you know the history of this monumnet with details?
Sabes la historia de este monumentos en detalle?
sabase laa istoria daya-stey mônumāntās ān detaye ?
सावेस ला इस्तोरिया दे एस्ते मोनूमेन्तोस एन बुदेताएय ?
11. How old it is?
Cúantos anos tiene?

Kuánto anos ti-a-nay ?
कुआन्तोस आन्योस तिएने

12. Was the king assassinated?
Fue asesinado el ray?
Fûe aasaysiinado l rayii.
फुए आसेसिनादो एल रई।

13. Did the queen die a natural death?
Tuvo la reina una muerte natural?
Tûvo laa raina ûna muarte natural ?
तुवो लो रेइना उना मुएरते नातूराल ?

14. Did the prince rule after the king's death?
Reinaba el principe despues de la muerte del rey?
Rainaba l prîncipe daspûes da laa muarte dri rei.
रेइनाबा एल प्रिन्सीपे देसपूएस दे ला मूएरते देल रेई ?

15. How many wives did he have?
Cúantas mujeres tenía?
Kuántas mukhāras tānîa.
कुआन्तास मूरवेरेस तेनिया ?

16. Tell me the exact period of his rule.
Dime el periodo exacto de su reinado.
dimayl páriodo áxacto dāy su reînado.
दिमे एल पेरियोदो एक्सातो दे सू रेइनादो।

17. Did he have any brothers?
Tenía hermanos?
tánîa ármanos ?

तेनिया एरमानोस ?

18. Was he enthroned during his father's life time itself?
Fue coronado durante la vida de su padre?
fua kōrōnaado durante laa vîda da su padre.
फूए कोरमान्दो दूरान्ते ला विदा दे सू पादरे ?

19. Who was the actual heir?
Quién fue el heredero verdadero?
kiân fuā l ēredāro vardaad-ero ?
किएन फूए एल ऐरेदेरो वेरदादेरो ?

20. Why does this arch stand separately?
porqué este arco está seperado?
porkê aste arko astâ sāperadōi?
पोरके एस्ते आरको एसता सेपेरादे?

21. Let's now enter the main structure.
vmos a entrar la estructura principal.
vamōos āa antrar laa āstruktura prîncîpal.
वामोस आ एन्तरार ला एसत्रूकतूरा प्रिनसिपाल।

22. Let's choose the right path.
Varmos a coger el camino corecto.
Vamōos aa kokhār l kamino korākto.
वामोस आ कोरवेर एल कामीनो कोरेक्तो।

23. Do we have to ascend any staircases?
Tenemos que subir algo escalera?
tanamos ka sûbir aalgōo ascalara ?
तेनेमोस के सूबीर आलो एस्कालेरा ?

24. Roughly how many steps?
Más o menos ?cuántos pasos?

Mâas o manos ? kûantōos pasōs ?
मास ओ मेनोस कुआन्तोस पासोस ?

25. Is it a one way route?
?Es una calle de dirección unica?
as ûna caya da dirakciôn oonikaa ?
एस उना काये दे दिरेक्सियोन अूनीका।

26. Is the exit route rather tough?
Es la ruta de salida defícil?
es laa rûta dā sâiiida - dificil ?
एस ला रूता दे सालिदा–दिफीसील ?

27. Where does it open?
Dónde abre?
dōndê aabra ?
दोन्दे आबरे ?

28. Were any foreign engineers involved in this construction?
Fueron involucredes ingenieros extranjeros en esta construcción?
fuêron învlukradôs inkhāniarôs extran khāros n-staa-konstruk c-on ?
फूअेरोन इन इनवोलुकरादोस इनरवेनियेरोस एन एस्ता कोन्सत्रूक्सिओन ?

29. Can you read the inscription on this tomb?
Puedes leer la inscripción en esta tumba?
puādes lêer laa inskripeiôn an ásta tumba ?
पूएदेस लेएर ला इन्सक्रीयसीओन एन एस्ता तूम्बा ?

30. Tell me what it says?
Dime lo que dice

dimme lô ke dĭce.
दिमे लो के दिसे ?

31. Does this minarette singnify some thing special?
Significa algo special este minarete?
signifika aalgoo spācial āste minarāte ?
सिकूनीफीका आलगो एस्पेसियाल एस्ते मिनारेते ?

32. Is it necessary to ignite incense stick here?
Es necesario encender trozos de incienso?
as nācesario āncānder trosos dā inciānsos ?
एस नेसेसारिओ एनसेनदेर त्रोसोस दे इन सियेनसोस?

33. Where does this tunnel lead to?
Dónde va este túnel?
Dôndā vāa aste tûnal ?
दोन्दे वा एस्ते तूनेल

34. Was it constructed later on?
Fue construido mas tarde?
Fuê konstruidoo maas tāhday ?
फूए कोन्सतूईदो मास तारदे ?

35. Was the king liked by the people?
Le gustaba a la gente el rey?
Le gûstaba āa laa khente l rei ?
ले गुसताबा आ ला खेन्ते एल रेई ?

36. Can I see through that ventilator?
Puedo ver por esa ventilador?
puādo vār pôr āsa vāntilador ?
पूएदो वेर पोर एसा वेन्तोलादोर ?

37. What do you call this structure in SPANISH?
Cómo se llama esta estructura en SPANISH?

komo sā yama āsta āstructura an indi ?
कोमो से ल्यामा एस्ता एस्त्रूक्तूरा एन हिन्दी ?

38. And what is the name of this material?
qui es el nombre de este material?
kâ as l nombro da aste matarîal ?
के एस एल नोम्ब्रे दे एस्ते मातेरियाल

39. Can one reach outside the dome?
Se puede llegar afuera de cúpula?
sa puāde yāgar afuêraa dāycûpula ?
से पूएदे लयागार आफूएरा दे कूपूला ?

40. Are these walls hollow?
Son huecas estos paredes?
sôn huakas āstas paarādes ?
सोन अूएकास एस्तास पारेदेस ?

41. Are these really solid?
Son solidos estos?
sôn solîdos āstos ?
सोन सोलिदोस एस्तोस

42. Were these made deliberately so?
Fueron hechas así deliberadamente?
fuerôn āchos āasi dālîbrradamānte ?
फूएरोन एचास आसी देलिबेरादामेन्ते ?

43. How much time it took to complete?
Cúanto tardó para cumplirlo?
kûanto tardô parāa kumplirlo ?
कूआन्तो तारदो पारा कूम्पलोरलो।

44. Were local artists and laborers employed?
Fueron empleados los artistos y obreros locales?

fueron m-play-aados lōs r-tiistō dorayros lokaalace ?

फूएरोन एमपलेयादोस लास आर्तिस्तोस इ ओबरेरोस लोकालेस ?

45. Who was the chief architect?
Ouién fue el arquitecto principal?
kiān fûe l arkitekto principal ?
किएन फूए एल आर्कि तेक्तो प्रिंसिपाल ?

46. Whose statue is this?
De quien es esta estatua?
de kian ās asta astatûa ?
दे किएन एस एस्ता एस्तातूआ ?

47. Can I go into sanctum sanctorum of the temple?
Puedo entrar el sanctasanctorum del templo?
puado entrar l sanktasanktoram dāl tāmplo ?
पूएदो एन्तरार एल सान्कतासानकतोरस देल तेम्पलो ?

48. What material this is made of?
De qué material está hecho?
dā qkā matēriāl astá acho ?
दे के मातेरियाल एसता एचो ?

49. Which god does this temple belong to?
A qué dios pertenece este templo?
A kā diôs pārtānecās āste tômplu ?
आ के दियोस पेरतेनेसे एस्ते तेम्पलो ?

50. Do we have to take our shoes off?
Tenemos que quitarnos nuestros zapatos?
tanemos kê kitarnos nuestros sapatos ?
तेनेमोस के कितारनोस नुएस्त्रोस सापातोस ?

51. Is there some eating place here?
Hay un lugar de comer por aquí?
ai ûn lûgar dā komār por akî ?
आई उन लुगार दे कोमेर पोर आकी ?

52. Is the prasad given to everyone?
Se da el prasad al todo el mundo?
sa dâl prasad al tôdo l mûndo.
से दा एल प्रसाद आल तोदो एल मुन्दो ?

53. Is it palatable for a foreigner?
Es sabroso para un extranjero?
ās saabrôso pāra an āxtrankhero ?
एस साबरोसो पारा उन एस्त्रानखेरो ?

54. And adequate in quantity too?
Y bastante candidad tambien?
i baastanta kandidaad tambian ?
ई बासतान्ते कान्तीदाद ताम्बीएन ?

55. How far is the beach?
Cuánto lejos está la playa?
kuânto lekhos āstâ laa playa ?
कुआन्तो लेखोस एसता लापलाया

56. Does the management accept any monetary contributions?
Acepta la gestion las contribuciones monetarias?
ācāpta laa khestiôn las kontribucionās moneytaariaar.
आसेप्ता ला खेस्तियोन लास कोन्त्रिबुसियोनेस मोनेतारियास ?

57. Then, where is this counter?
Entonces ?dónde está mostrador?
āntonces ? Dôndá āstâ mostrador ?
एन्तोन्सेस दोन्दे एस्ता मोस्तरादोर ?

58. Can we hire swimming costume here?
Podemos alquilar el bañador?
Podemos alkilar l banadōor ?
पोदेमोस आलकिलार एल बान्यादोर ?

59. Is there facility for sun bathing?
Hay la facilidad de tomar el sol?
al laa phacilidād dā tomār l sol ?
आई ला फासीलीदाद दे तोमार एल सोल ?

60. Are only foreigners allowed?
Se permiten los extranjeros sólo?
sa pārmitān lôs āxtrānkheros sólo ?
से पेरमितेन लोस एसत्रान्खेरोस सोलो ?

61. How does one reach that island?
Cómo se llegaa esa isla?
komo sā yegaa āsa îsla ?
कोमो से ल्येगा आसा इसला ?

62. By steamer, motor boat or ferry?
Por vapor, por motora por barco?
Pôr vapôr. pôr motorâ pôr barko ?
पोर वापोर पोर मोतोरा ओ पोर बारको ?

63. Do you have any of your friends in Manali?
Tienes alguien de tus amigos en Manali?
Tianes alguiān dā tûs amigos an manali ?
तिऐनेस आलीगिरान दे तूसंआमीगो ए एन मनाली ?

64. Yes, we want to visit that hilly area also.
Si, queremos visitar las areas acidentadas
sî, qkārāmos visitoor lâs ārrās acîdentadas.
सी केरेमोस विसितार लास आरेआस आक्सिदेन्तादास।

65. Thank you very much for your excellent job.
Muchas gracias para tu trabajo excelente.
Mûchas graciaas para tû trabakho āxcelente.
मुचास ग्रासियास पारा तू त्राबारवो एक्सिलेन्ते।

66. Here is your fee…….keep the change.
Aquí tienes el pago,   toma el cambio.
Aki Tiānes l pago, toma el cambio.
आकी तिएनेस एल पागोए तोमा एल काम्बियो।

General sentences for every day use

1. Hello, how are you?
   Hola como estás?
   olāa ko-mo ēs-tāas ?
   ओला कोमो एसतास ?
2. I am fine.
   Estoy bien
   A-stoii B-N
   एस्तोई बिएन
3. Bring me +coffee.
   Traigame el cáfe.
   Trāa-ii-ga-mēe l kā-fēe
   त्राएगामें एल काफे
4. Stay there.
   Quedate alli.
   k-dāa-te āalee
   केदाते आ–ई
5. Come here.
   Venga aqui.
   Vēe-ngāa āakii
   बेंगा आकी
6. Go inside.
   Vaya adentro.

Vāa-yāa āadēentrō.
वाया आदेन्त्रो

7. Wait in the lawn.
Espere en el járdin.
ēes-pēe-ray n l khāardiin.
एसपेरे एन एल खारदिन

8. Meet at the gate.
Encuentre a la puerta.
n-koo-n-tray āa lāa pooēertā
एन्कूएन्त्रे आ ला पुसरता

9. Walk on the pavemnet.
Ande sobre el pavimento.
āanday sōbray l pāaviimen-tō.
आन्दे सोबेर एल पावीमेन्तो

10. It is not a parking place.
No es un aparcamiento.
No s oon āaparkāamii-n-tō
नो एस उन अपारकामिएन्तो

11. The pen is in the box.
La pluma está en cajón.
lāa ploomāa s-tāa n kakhōn
ला पलूमा एस्ता एल काखोन

12. Your shoe is under the table.
Tu zapato está debajo de la mesa.
Tû sapâtōo āstâ dābapkhô dā laa masāa.
तू सापातो एस्ता देबाखो दे ला मेसा

13. The green stripe is below the white one.
Le saya verde está debajode la blanca.

la sāayāa vārdê āstāa dābāakho dā laa blaan-ka
ला साया बेर्दे एस्ता देबाखो दे ला बलान्का

14. Lift the ball from the ground.
Levante la pelota del suelo.
lavantê laa pālōotâ dāl sûeloo
लेवान्ते ला पेलोता देल सूएलो

15. Take it.
Tomalo.
Tôomalo .
तोमालो

16. Give me the paper.
Dame el papel.
daamā l papāl.
दा.मे एल पापेल

17. It is cold outside.
Hace frio afuera.
acê phrîo aaphuerāa
आसे फ्रिओ आफुएरा

18. It is rather humid inside.
Está húmido adentro.
āstāa ûmiido aadāntrōo
एस्ता अूमीदो आदेन्त्रो

19. It still appears dirty.
Parece sucio todavía.
paarecā sûcioo todavîa.
पारसे सुसिओ तोदाविया

20. She has not come yet.

No ha venido ella todavia.
No, a, bāniido yaa todavîa.
नो आ वेनिदो एआ तोदाविया

21. Yes, now it appears clean.
Sí, ahora parece limpio.
Sî aôra parecā liimpîo.
सी, आओरा पारेसे लिम्पियो

22. Go upstairs.
Venga abajo.
Bānga aabaakho.
वेन्गा आबारवो

23. Come downstairs
Venga debajo.
Bānga dābaakho.
वेन्गा देबाखो

24. I want a washer man.
necesito un lavandero.
nācesîto ûn laavaandarô
नेसेसितो उन लावान्देरो

25. Is there a laundary nearby?
Hay un lavandería acerca?
ay ûn laa vaandārîa aacārca ?
आई उन लावान्देरिया आसेरका ?

26. Can she iron this shirt well?
Puede ella planchar bien la camisa?
puāde yaa plaānchāar bîen laa caamisaa ?
पुएदे एआ प्लानचार विएन ला कामोसा ?

27. Call her quickly.

L Lamale a ella en seguida?
yamale aa yia an sāguîdaa.
ल्यामाले आ एआ एन सेगिदा

28. It is getting late.
Está tarde.
astâ taarde.
एसता तारदे

29. It is quite early.
Está muy temprqno.
astá mui tāmptaano
एसता मुई तेमपरानो

30. Run faster
Corre rapidamecte.
korrā raapidamentee
कार्रे रापिदामेन्ते

31. Walk slowly.
Anda l'entamente.
aāndāa lāntamānte.
आन्दा लेन्तामेन्ते

32. The newspaper is on the bed.
El periódico está en la cama.
l pāriôdicōo astâ en laa caamaa.
एल पेरीओदिको एसता एन ला कामा

33. The dictionary is above the magazine.
El diccionario está sobre la revista.
l diccionariô astá sôbre laa ravista.
एल दिक्सियोनारियो एसता सोबरे ला रेविस्ता

34. The post office is in front.

La casa de correo está adelanta.
laa casa da korrao astâ aadelaanta.
ला कासा दे कोर्रेयो एसता आदेलान्ता

35. What lies behind it?
Qué está detrás?
kê astâ drtraas ?
के एसता दे त्रास ?

36. There is a banyan tree beside the mosque.
Hay un árbol de banyan al lado de la mezqúita.
ay ûr aarbôol dā baanian aal laado dā laa meskîta.
आई उन आरबोल दे बनयान आल लादो दे ला मेस्किता।

37. Are you from Oriental Travels?
Erés de oriental travels?
ārâs da oriantaal trâvels ?
एरेस दे ओरिएन्ताल ट्रेवल्स ?

38. Will this telephonic talk do?
Bastará esta conversación telefonica?
Baastaaraâ astâ konvārsaciôn telaphœnicaa ?
बास्तारा एसता कोन्वेरसासियोन टेलेफोनिका

39. We want to visit Nainital.
Queremos visitar Nainital.
keremos bisitaâr Nainital.
केरेमोस विसितार नैनीताल

40. For four adults.
Preporcionas viajes organisadas?
pre pôrcionaas viakhes organîsados ?

प्रेपोरसियोनास वियाखेस ओरगानीसादास ?

41. For adults.
Sólo para adultos.
sôolo pârâ aadultos.
सोलो पारा आदूल्तोस

42. No, there are no children.
No hay niños.
No, ai, ninos.
नो, आई निन्योस

43. Yes, no one is under twenty five.
Sí, nadie tiene menos de 25 años.
sî, nâadie tiāne menôs dā 25 anos.
सी, नादिए तिएने मेनोस दे 25 आनयोस

44. For four days including up and own jouney?
Para cuatro dias incluso viajes de ida y vuelta?
pârâ kuatroo ďiias inkluso viajes dā ida y buelta.
पारा कूआत्रो दियास इन्कलूसो वियायेस दे इदा ई भूएल्ता।

45. Including all the meals?
Incluso todas las comidas?
Incluso todôas laas côomidas ?
इनकलुसो तोदास लास कोमिदास

46. Excluding lunches?
Sin almuerzos?
Sîn aalmuer sos ?
सिन आलमूएर सोस

47. You are asking for too much.

Estás pidiendo demasiado.
astâs pîdiendo, dēmasiado.
एसता पिदि एन्दो देमासियासे

48. No, it's not reasonable.
No, no es razonable.
no, no as rasonable.
नो, नो एस रासोनाबले

49. Which vehicle will you provide?
Qué vehículo vas a proporcionar?
ké, vehîculoo bâs aa prôporciônar ?
के भेहीकूलो वास आ प्रोपेरसिओनार ?

50. Yes, an A.C.Qualis will be better.
Sí, un coche aire condicionado será mejor.
sî ûn koche aîre condiciianaadoo sāra māphor.
सी उन कोचे आएरे कोनदिसिओनादो सेरामेफारे।

51. It is a public telephone booth?
Es una cabina telefonica publica?
as ûna cabina têlephónik pûblika ?
एस उना काबीना तेलेफोनिका पुब्लिका ?

52. Can I make an ISD call from here?
Puedo hacer una llamada internacional de aquí?
puadôo acêr ûna yamadaa intārnacional dā akî?
पूएदो आसेर उना यामादा इन्तेरनासियोनाल दे आकी?

53. And local call s well?
También las llamadas locales?
Tambiên laas yaamaādaās lokalās ?
ताम्बीएन लास ल्यामादास लोकालेस ?

54. Do you have internet facility also?
También tienes la facilidad de internet?
Tambiên tiēnes laa facilidaad de intêrnêt
ताम्बीएन तिऐनेस ला फासीलीदाद दे इंतेरनेत ?

55. Can I check my E-mail here?
Puādo chequear mi e-mail aqui?
puadoo chēe-k-aar mî e-mâil akî ?
पूऐदो चेकेआर मी ई–मेल आकी ?

56. At what rate you charge for net surfing?
Quéprecio cobras para navegar el internet?
á ka prêcio kobras para navêgar al intêrnêt?
ए का प्रीसीयो कोब्रास पारा नावेगार एल इनतरनेत ?

57. So you sell antiques....?
Entonces ?vendes antigüedades?
antonces, bendâs antigiiedēades ?
एन्तोन्सेस वेन्देस आन्तीगुएदादेस ?

58. And modern art works?
Y las obras modernas?
i laas obraâs môdernas ?
ई लास ओबारास मोदेरनास ?

59. How much is that silicon cap?
Cuánto cuesta está gorra de ceda?
Kuânto kuestaā āstá gorra de cêdaa ?
कुआन्तो कुएस्ता एस्ता गोर्रा दे सेदा ?

60. No, the red one behind the orange one.
No, la roja detrás de la naranja.
No, laa rokha dātras de la narankha.
नो ला रोखा देत्रास दे ला नारन्खा.

61. My god, is it so expensive?
Dios mio es tan caro.
Dios mío as tân câaro.
दियोस मियो एस तान कारो।

62. Some thing cheaper?
Algo barato?
Algo báaráato.
आलगो बारातो

63. Does this bronze piece qualify as an antique?
También esa pieza de bronze es una antigüedad?
Tambiên āsa piêsa dā bronse ās ûna antiguediaad.
ताम बोएन एसा पिएसा दे ब्रोंसे एस उना आनतीगुएदाद ?

64. O. K., pack it.
Vale , empaquetalo.
Bale, āmpakātaalo.
बाले एम्पाके तालो।

65. Don't delay.
No tardes.
no, târdês.
नो तारेदेस

66. Tell him to keep his fingers off the piece.
Dile que no toque la pieza.
dila ke no toke la piiza.
दीले के नो तोके ला पीएजा।

67. My shoes need polish.
Mis zapatos necesitan pulír.

mis sapatos necesitañ pooliir.
मीस सामातोस नेसेसितान पूलीर

68. I need a hair cut.
Necesito un corte de pelo.
necesitōo ûno kôrtā dā pāloo.
नेसेसीतो उन कोरते दे पेलो।

69. Will I have to go to saloon?
Tandré que ir al salón?
tāndrâ all saloôn ?
तेन्द्रे के ईर आल सालोन

70. What do you mean?
Qúe quieres decir?
kā kiārâs dācîr ?
के क्यिरेस देसिर ?

71. Why are you worried?
Porqué estás preocupado?
Pôrkā astâs prāocûapado ?
पोरके एसतास प्रेओकुपादो ?

72. How do you cook it?
Cómo lo cocinas?
komo lô côcinaas ?
कोमो लो कोसिनास ?

73. Where did you get it?
Dónde lo conseguiste?
Dônda lô consaguistâ?
दोन्दे लो कोन्सेगिस्ते ?

74. Which of these is yours?
Cuál de estos es tuyo?

kuâl dā āstos ās tûyo ?
कुआल दे एस्तोस एस तूयो ?

75. When do we go?
A qué hora vamos?
a qkê orâ bamôs ?
आ के ओरा भामोस।

76. Shrpen this pencil.
Saca punta a este lápiz.
saka pûnta aā āstē lâpis ?
साकापून्ता आ एस्ते लापीस।

77. What is the matter?
que pasa?
kê pāasāa ?
के पासा ?

78. It does not sound good.
No suena bien.
No sûena bian.
नो सूएना बिएन

79. I am ready for last two hours.
Estoy listo hace las ultimas dos horas.
astoi lîsto ace laas ûltimœas dôs oras.
एस्तोई लिस्तो आसे लास उलतोमास दोस होरास।

80. I don't believe it.
No lo creo.
नो लो क्रेओ।

Spanish Vocabulary

1.	a; one	un(o), una	A; one	*oon*	उन
2.	above, over, upon; about	Sobre	above, over, upon; about	*so-bre*	सोब्रे
3.	advise	aconsejar	advise	*àa kón sée khāar*	आकोनसेखार
4.	afternoon	Tarde	afternoon	*taa-r-de*	तारदे
5.	aid, help	ayudar	aid, help	*āa-u-dāar*	आयुदार
6.	all, every	Todo	all, every	*to-do*	तोदो
7.	almost	Casí	almost	*kaasii*	कासि

8.	already	Ya	already	*ya*	या
9.	also	también	also	*taa-m-bien*	ताम्बिएन
10.	although	aunque	although	*aoon-K*	आउनके
11.	always	siempre	always	*si-empre*	सिएम्परे
12.	American	Americano	American	*āamayrrükano*	आमेरिकानो
13.	and	Y	and	*e*	ई
14.	announcement	anuncio	announcemen t	*āanuncüo*	आनुन्सीओ
15.	answer, reply	contestar	answer, reply	*kōn-tess-tāar*	कोन्तेस्तार
16.	appear, seem	parecer	appear, seem	*pāaraysēer*	पारेसेर
17.	approach, near to	acercarse	approach, near to	*āa-seerkaar sée*	आसेकारसे
18.	April	abril	April	*āa-brül*	आबरील
19.	area	extensión	area	*Aks-tēen-c-on*	एक्सतेन्सिओन
20.	arrive	llegar	arrive	*yegāar*	ल्यागार

21.	Art	arte	art	*āatēe*	आरते
22.	Art gallery	galleria	art gallery	*gaaleyriya*	गालेरिआ
23.	artist	artista	artist	*āatiista*	आरतिस्ता
24.	As much; so much	tanto	as much; so much	*taa-n-to*	तान्तो
25.	as, like, how buy	como	as, like, how buy	*kōmō*	कोमो
26.	as, so,	Tan	as, so,	*taan*	तान
27.	Ask	preguntar	ask	*praygoontaar*	प्रेगून्तार
28.	Ask for, order	pedir	ask for, order	*paydiir*	पेदिर
29.	At once, immediately	seguida	at once, immediately	*se-gidāa*	सेगिदा
30.	at, in, to	A	at, in, to	*ā*	आ
31.	attend, be present at	asistir	attend, be present at	*āasisteer*	आसिस्तिर

32.	augment, increase	aumnetar	augment, increase	*āaoomentāar*	आउमेनतार
33.	August	agosto	August	*āagōstō*	आगोस्तो
34.	auto, car	auto	auto, car	*āaootō*	आउतो
35.	autumn	oveja	autumn	*o-vēe-khāa*	ओवेखो
36.	awaken	despertar	awaken	*des-per-tāar*	देस्पेरतार
37.	back of, behind	detrás de	back of, behind	*day-trāas dey*	देत्रास दे
38.	bad	malo	bad	*māalō*	मालो
39.	badly	mal	badly	*māal*	माल
40.	baker	panadero	baker	*paanaadeyro*	पानादेरो
41.	bakery	panaderí*a*	bakery	*paaradeyriya*	पानादेरिया
42.	bank	banco	bank	*bāan-ko*	बान्को
43.	bathroom	cuarto de baño	bathroom	*kooarto de baño*	कुआर्तरे दे बान्यो

44.	Be	estar	be	*ace-tāar*	एस्तार
45.	Be	ser	be	*ser*	सेर
46.	be able, can	poder	be able, can	*pōdeyr*	पोदेर
47.	be enough, quite	bastar	be enough, quite	*bāas-tāar*	बासतार
48.	Be glad to	alegrarse	be glad to	*āalay-grāar-say*	आलेगरारसे
49.	beautiful	hermoso	beautiful	*ērmo-so*	एरमासो
50.	because	porque	because	*pōrkay*	पोरके
51.	bedroom	alcoba	bedroom	*āalkōbāa*	आलकोबा
52.	before	antes de	before	*āantess dey*	आन्तेस दे
53.	begin	empezar	begin	*M-pay-sāar*	एम्पेसार
54.	believe, think	creer	believe, think	*kreyr*	क्रेएर
55.	better	mejor	better	*maykhor*	मेखोर
56.	between, among	entre	between, among	*n-tray*	एन्त्रे

57.	bill	cuento	bill	*kooentāa*	कुएन्ता
58.	bird	pájaro	bird	*pāakhar*	पाखारो
59.	black	negro	black	*naygro*	नेगरो
60.	blackboard	pizarra	blackboard	*piizārrāa*	पिसारा
61.	blue	azul	blue	*āasool*	आसूल
62.	book	libro	book	*lii-bro*	लिब्रो
63.	bookseller	librero	bookseller	*librey-ro*	लिबरेरो
64.	bookstore	librería	bookstore	*libereyriya*	लिबरेरिया
65.	bottle	botella	bottle	*botāy-ya*	बोतेत्या
66.	bread	pan	bread	*paan*	पान
67.	breakfast	desayunarse	breakfast	*dey-saa-u-naar-say*	देसायुनारसे
68.	breakfast	desayuno	breakfast	*dey-saa-u-no*	देसायुनो
69.	bring	traer	bring	*tráa-er*	त्राएर
70.	broad, wide	ancho	broad, wide	*āancho*	आन्चो

71.	brother(sister)	hermano	brother(sister)	*ēer-māa-no*	एरमानो
72.	but	pero	but	*payro*	पेरो
73.	but, except	sino	but, except	*sino*	सिनो
74.	butter	mantequilla	butter	*mante-kiya*	मान्तेकिया
75.	buy	comprar	buy	*kōm-praar*	कोम्प्रार
76.	by, in, at, for, through	por	by, in, at, for, through	*pōr*	पोर
77.	call	llamar	call	*yamaar*	ल्यामार
78.	capital	capital	capital	*kaapeetaal*	कापिताल
79.	careful	cuidadoso	careful	*kooiidāadō-so*	कुइदादोसो
80.	carry	llevár	carry	*yevāar*	ल्येवार
81.	chair	silla	chair	*si-lya*	सिल्या
82.	chalk	tiza	chalk	*tee-saa*	तिसा
83.	Charles	carlos	Charles	*kaarlōs*	कारलोस
84.	chat, talk	charlar·	chat, talk	*chāarlāar*	चारलार

85.	cheap	barato	cheap	*barāatō*	बारातो
86.	cheese	queso	cheese	*ke-so*	केसो
87.	child	niño	child	*niinyo*	निन्यो
88.	church	iglesia	church	*ig-lay-siya*	इग्लेसिआ
89.	cigar	cigarro	cigar	*c-gāa-rō*	सिगार्रो
90.	city	ciudad	city	*c-u-dāad*	सिऊदाद
91.	class grade	nota	class grade	*no-tāa*	नोता
92.	class; kind, sort	clase	class; kind, sort	*klaasay*	क्लास
93.	climate	clima	climate	*kleemāa*	क्लीमा
94.	close	cerrar	close	*ser-aar*	सेर्रार
95.	clothing	ropa	clothing	*ro-pāa*	रोपा
96.	coal	carbón	coal	*kaarbone*	कारबोन
97.	coast, shore	costa	coast, shore	*kōs-tāa*	कोस्ता
98.	coffee, Café	café	coffee, Café	*kāafēe*	काफे

99.	cold	frío	cold	*free-o*	फ्रिओ
100.	color	còlor	color	*kō-lōr*	कोलोर
101.	come	venir	come	*ve-neer*	वेनिर
102.	comedy, play	comedia	comedy, play	*kō-maydiya*	कोमेदिया
103.	command	mandar	command	*māandāar*	मानदार
104.	commerce	comercio	commerce	*kō-mayr-C-D*	कोमेरसियो
105.	common, usual	común	common, usual	*ko-moon*	कोमून
106.	conversation	conversación	conversation	*kōn-versasü-on*	कोन्वेरसासिओ न
107.	cool	fresco	cool	*freskō*	फ्रेस्को
108.	copper	cobre	copper	*kōbrey*	कोब्रे
109.	copy	copiar	copy	*kō-pee-r*	कोपिआर
110.	corn	maíz	corn	*māaiz*	माएस
111.	correctly	Correctament	correctly	*kō-rēektāmentēe*	कोरेक्तामेन्ते

		e			
112.	cost	costar	cost	*kōstāar*	कोस्तार
113.	cotton	algodón	cotton	*āalgodōn*	आलगोदोन
114.	count, relate, tell	contar	count, relate, tell	*kōntāar*	कोन्तार
115.	country	país	country	*paa-iis*	पाइस
116.	courteous	cortés	courteous	*kōrtess*	कोरतेस
117.	cousin	primo	cousin	*preemo*	प्रिमो
118.	cow	vaca	cow	*vaa-kaa*	भाका
119.	cup	taza	cup	*taa-zo*	तासा
120.	dance	bailar	dance	*bye-lāar*	बैलार
121.	dear, expensive	caro	dear, expensive	*kāarō*	कारो
122.	December	diciembre	December	*dii-c-m-brey*	दिसिएम्ब्रे
123.	describe	describir	describe	*des-krii-biir*	देस्क्रीबीर

124.	desire	gana	desire	*gāanāa*	गाना
125.	dictionary	diccionario	dictionary	*dik-c-o-naa-riyo*	दिक्सियोनारियो
126.	difference	diferencia	difference	*dii-fēe-ren-c-āa*	दिफेरेसिन्या
127.	different	diferente	different	*dii-fēe-ren-tēe*	दिफेरेन्ते
128.	difficulty	dificultad	difficulty	*diifii-cool-tāad*	दिफीकुल्ताद
129.	diligent	diligente	diligent	*diliikhentēei*	दिलीखेन्ते
130.	diligent	distinto	diligent	*diis-tiin-tō*	दिस्तीन्तो
131.	dining room	comedor	dining room	*kō-may-dōr*	कोमेदोर
132.	distinguish	distinguir	distinguish	*diis-tin-gür*	दिस्तिंगीर
133.	doctor, physician	médico	doctor, physician	*maydiiko*	मेदिको
134.	dollar	dólar	dollar	*dōlāar*	दोलार
135.	door	puerta	door	*pooertáa*	पुएरता
136.	doubt	dudar	doubt	*dōo-dāar*	दूदार

137.	drama, play	drama	drama, play	*drāa-māa*	ड्रामा
138.	dramatist	dramaturgo	dramatist	*drāa-māa-tur-go*	ड्रामातूरगो
139.	dress oneself, dress	vestirse	dress oneself, dress	*ves-teer-se*	वेस्तिरसे
140.	dress; clothes	vestido	dress; clothes	*ves-teedo*	वेस्तिदो
141.	drink	beber	drink	*bay-bēer*	बेबेर
142.	during	durante	during	*dōo-raan-tēė*	दुरान्ते
143.	each, every	cada	each, every	*kaada*	कादा
144.	early	temprano	early	*tem-prāano*	तेम्प्रानो
145.	easy	fácil	easy	*fāa-sil*	फासील
146.	eat	comer	eat	*kō-may-er*	कोमेर
147.	eight	ocho	eight	*o-cho*	ओचो
148.	eighty	ochenta	eighty	*o-chen-tāa*	ओचेन्ता
149.	eleven	once	eleven	*own-say*	ओन्से
150.	eleven	oro	eleven	*o-row*	ओरो

151.	employ, use	emplear	employ, use	*M-play-āar*	एम्प्लेआर
152.	end	fin	end	*fiin*	फिन
153.	end, finish	acabar	end, finish	*akāabar*	आकाबार
154.	end, finish	terminar	end, finish	*ter-meenaar*	तेरमिनार
155.	England	Inglaterra	England	*Ing-lāa-tērrāa*	इन्गलातेर्रा
156.	English	ingles	English	*ing-lace*	इन्गलेस
157.	enjoy	gozar	enjoy	*go-sar*	गोसार
158.	enormous	enorme	enormous	*n-ōr-may*	एनोरमे
159.	enough, quite	bastante	enough, quite	*baastaantēe*	बास्तान्ते
160.	enter	entrar	enter	*n-tnāar*	एन्त्रार
161.	entire, whole	entero	entire, whole	*n-tero*	एन्तेरो
162.	Europe	Europa	Europe	*A-oorōpāa*	एउरोपा
163.	every day	día	every day	*diiya*	दिया
164.	examination	examen	examination	*A-kjaa-men*	एक्सामेन
165.	example	ejemplo	example	*A-khem-plo*	एखेम्प्लो

166.	excuse, excuse me	dispensar	excuse, excuse me	*diis-pen-sāar*	दिस्पेन्सार
167.	exercise	ejercicio	exercise	*A-kher-c-c-o*	एखेरसिसीओ
168.	explain	explicar	explain	*aks-plii-kaar*	एक्सप्लीकार
169.	factory	fábrica	factory	*fāabriika*	फाब्रीका
170.	fall	caer	fall	*kāaēer*	काएर
171.	family	familia	family	*fāa-mii-liigo*	फामीलिआ
172.	famous	famoso	famous	*fāa-mō-sō*	फामोसो
173.	far from	lejos de	far from	*laykhos dey*	लेखोस दे
174.	farm	hacienda	farm	*aa-c-n-dāa*	आसिएन्दा
175.	farmer	campesino	farmer	*kāampayseeno*	काम्पेसीनो
176.	father	padre	father	*pāadrey*	पादरे
177.	favor	favor	favor	*fāa-vōr*	फावोर
178.	fear	temer	fear	*ti-mer*	तेमेर
179.	February	febrero	February	*feb-re-ro*	फेबरेरो

180.	feel, regret	sentir	feel, regret	*sen-tir*	सेन्तिर
181.	festival, holiday	fiesta	fẹstival, holiday	*feeacetāa*	फिएस्ता
182.	field, country	campo	field, country	*kāampō*	काम्पो
183.	fifteen	quince	fifteen	*ki-nse*	किन्से
184.	fifty	cincuenta	fifty	*sin-kooentāa*	सिन्कुएन्ता
185.	fig	higo	fig	*ii-go*	ईगो
186.	fig tree	higuera	fig tree	*iis-tōriya*	ईगेरा
187.	find	hallar	find	*aa-yaar*	आल्यार
188.	first	primero	first	*preemayro*	प्रिरेमेरो
189.	five	cinco	five	*sim-kō*	सिन्को
190.	floor	suelo	floor	*soo-e-lo*	सूएलो
191.	floor, story	piso	floor, story	*piiso*	पिसो
192.	flower	flor	flower	*flō-or*	फ्लोर
193.	follow, go on,	seguir	follow, go on,	*se-guieer*	सेगिर

	continue		continue		
194.	foot	pie	foot	*piiye*	पिए
195.	for, to, in order to	para	for, to, in order to	*para*	पारा
196.	foreign	extranjero	foreign	*Aks-traanphero*	एस्त्रांखेरो
197.	forest	bosque	forest	*bōs-K*	बोस्के
198.	forget	olvidar	forget	*ol-viidāar*	ओल्विदार
199.	forty	cuarenta	forty	*kooarentāa*	कुआरेन्ता
200.	fountain pen	plumafuente	fountain pen	*ploomafoo-n-tēe*	प्लूमाफूएन्ते
201.	four	cuatro	four	*kooatro*	कुआत्रो
202.	fourteen	catorce	fourteen	*kaatōrsay*	कातोरसे
203.	France	Francia	France	*frāan-ciia*	फ्रांसीआ
204.	French	francés	French	*frāan-ces*	फ्रान्सेस
205.	Friday	viernes	Friday	*vee-e-rnes*	विएरनेस
206.	friend	amigo	friend	*āamügo*	आमिगो

207.	from, since	desde	from, since	*dēes-dey*	देस्दे
208.	fruit	fruta	fruit	*froo tāa*	फ्रूता
209.	full	lleno	full	*yeno*	ल्येनो
210.	gain	ganar	gain	*gāanāar*	गानार
211.	garden	jardín	garden	*khaardiin*	खारदिन
212.	German	alemán	German	*aalaymāan*	आलेमान
213.	Germany	alemania	Germany	*aalaymaannüya*	आलेमानिया
214.	get into a train	subir	get into a train	*soo-bir*	सूबीर
215.	get tired	cansarse	get tired	*kāansāarsay*	कान्सारसे
216.	get up	levantarse	get up	*layvaantāarsay*	लेवान्तारसे
217.	give	dar	give	*dāar*	दार
218.	glass	vaso	glass	*vaa-so*	भासो
219.	glove	guante	glove	*gooaantēe*	गुआन्ते
220.	go	Ir	go	*eer*	इर

221.	go down	bajar	go down	*bakhāar*	बाखार
222.	go out, leave	salir	go out, leave	*sāa-lir*	सालिर
223.	go to bed	acostarse	go to bed	*ācōstāarsay*	आकोस्तारसे
224.	gold	otro	gold	*o-trō*	ओत्रो
225.	good	bueno	good	*booēeno*	बुऐनो
226.	good-bye	adiós	good-bye	*āa-dü-os*	आदियोस
227.	grammar	gramática	grammar	*graa-māa-tii-ka*	ग्रामातिका
228.	grape	uva	grape	*oo-wa*	ऊवा
229.	green	verde	green	*ver-de*	वेर्दे
230.	half	medio	half	*maydii-o*	मेदियो
231.	hand	mano	hand	*māano*	मानो
232.	happy	feliz	happy	*fe-liis*	फेलीस
233.	happy, gay	alegre	happy, gay	*āalaygray*	आलेगरे
234.	hard difficult	defícil	hard difficult	*diifiisil*	दिफीसील
235.	hardly,	apenas	hardly,	*aapaynaas*	आपेनास

	scarcely		scarcely		
236.	haste, hurry	prisa	haste, hurry	*preesāa*	प्रिसा
237.	hat	sombrero	hat	*som-bre-ro*	सोम्ब्रेरो
238.	hat shop	sombrería	hat shop	*somber-riāa*	सोम्ब्रेरिया
239.	have	haber	have	*aabēer*	आबेर
240.	have a good time	divertirse	have a good time	*dii-vēer-tiirsay*	दिवेरतीरसे
241.	have, hold	tener	have, hold	*te-nèr*	तेनेर
242.	he, it	Él	he, it	*l*	एल
243.	head	cabeza	head	*kaabaysa*	काबेसा
244.	health	salud	health	*sāa-lood*	सालूद
245.	healthy, healthful	sano	healthy, healthful	*sāa-no*	सानो
246.	hear, understand	entender	hear, understand	*n-tēen-dēer*	एन्तेंदेर

247.	heat	calor	heat	*kāalōr*	कालोर
248.	hen	gallina	hen	*gaiina*	गाल्यीना
249.	here	aquí	here	*āakü*	आकी
250.	high	alto	high	*āal-tō*	आलतो
251.	himself, herself, yourself, themselves	se	himself, herself, yourself, themselves	*se*	से
252.	his, her, its, your, their	su	his, her, its, your, their	*soo*	सू
253.	his, hers, yours, theirs	suyo	his, hers, yours, theirs	*soo-yo*	सूयो
254.	Historical	histórico	historical	*iistōriiko*	इस्तोरिका
255.	history	historia	history	*iis-tōriya*	इस्तोरिआ
256.	Hope	esperar	hope	*acepyraar*	एस्पेरार

257.	Horse	caballo	horse	*kabayo*	काबाय्यो
258.	Hot	caliente	hot	*kāaliyentēe*	कालिएन्ते
259.	Hotel	hotel	hotel	*otēel*	ओतेल
260.	hour	hora	hour	*ora*	ओरा
261.	house, home	casa	house, home	*kāasa*	कासा
262.	how much	cúanto	how much	*kooantō*	कुआंतो
263.	hundred	ciento	hundred	*C-N-tō*	सिएन्ता
264.	Hunger	hambre	hunger	*aam-brey*	आम्ब्रे
265.	I	yo	I	*yo*	यो
266.	If	si	if	*si*	सी
267.	important	importante	important	*impōrtaantēe*	इम्पोरतान्ते
268.	impossible	imposible	impossible	*impōseeblay*	इम्पोसीब्ले
269.	In front of	delante de	in front of	*deylaantēe*	देलान्ते दे
270.	In spite of	pesar	in spite of	*ppaysaar*	पेसार
271.	in, into, at, by,	en	in, into, at,	*n*	एन

	on		by, on		
272.	inhabitant	habitante	inhabitant	*aabiitaantēe*	आबीतान्ते
273.	ink	tinta	ink	*tee-ntāa*	तिन्ता
274.	intelligent	inteligente	intelligent	*intēeliikhentēe*	इन्तेलेखेन्ते
275.	interest	interesar	interest	*intēeraysaar*	इन्तेरेसार
276.	interesting	intersante	interesting	*intēeresāantēe*	इन्तेरेसान्ते
277.	investigate	investigar	investigate	*investiigāar*	इन्भेस्तीगार
278.	iron	hierro	iron	*ii-erro*	इएर्रो
279.	January	enero	January	*n-a-ro*	एनेरो
280.	John	Juan	John	*khooāam*	खूआन
281.	July	Julio	July	*khoolii-o*	खूलियो
282.	June	junio	June	*khoonii-o*	खूनियो
283.	kindness	bondad	kindness	*bone-daad*	बोनदाद
284.	king	rey	king	*ree-i*	रेई
285.	kitchen,	cocina	kitchen,	*kō-c-nāa*	कोसीना

	cuisine		cuisine		
286.	know	conocer	know	*kōno-ser*	कोनोसेर
287.	know	saber	know	*sāa-ber*	साबेर
288.	language	lengua	language	*layngooāa*	लेन्गुआ
289.	large	grande	large	*grāandey*	ग्रान्दे
290.	larger	mayor	larger	*māa-yōor*	मायोर
291.	las	noticias	las	*notii-c-āas*	नोतिसियास
292.	last	último	last	*oo-l-teemo*	उल्तिमो
293.	laugh	reír	laugh	*ree-ir*	रेइर
294.	lawyer	abogado	lawyer	*āabōgāa dō*	आबोगादो
295.	lazy	perezoso	lazy	*payraysoso*	पेरेसोसो
296.	lead	plomo	lead	*plō-mō*	पलोमो
297.	learn	aprender	learn	*āaprēendēer*	आपरेनदेर
298.	less	menos	less	*mēen-os*	मेनोस
299.	lesson	lección	lesson	*lec-c-own*	लेकसियोन

300.	letter	carta	letter	*kāartāa*	कार्ता
301.	life	vida	life	*vee-dāa*	विदा
302.	line	línea	line	*lee-nay-āa*	लिनेयो
303.	list	lista	list	*lee-stāa*	लिस्ता
304.	listen, listen to	escuchar	listen, listen to	*s-koo-chaar*	एस्कुएला
305.	literary	literario	literary	*lee-tēe-rāariyo*	लितेरारियो
306.	literature	literatura	literature	*lee-teratuāa*	लितेरातूरा
307.	little	poco	little	*pōkō*	पोको
308.	live	vivir	live	*vee-veer*	विविर
309.	living room	sala	living room	*sāa-lāa*	साला
310.	long	largo	long	*lāar-go*	लारगो
311.	look at	mirar	look at	*miiraar*	मिरार
312.	look for, seek	buscar	look for, seek	*boos-kāar*	बुस्कार
313.	lose	perder	lose	*pērdeyr*	पेरदेर

314.	love	amar	love	*āamaar*	आमार
315.	low	bajo	low	*báaplo*	बाखो
316.	magnificent	magnífico	magnificent	*māaniifiiko*	मागनीफिको
317.	make	hacer	make	*aa-ser*	आसेर
318.	man	hombre	man	*ōm-brey*	ओम्ब्रे
319.	manner	modo	manner	*mōodō*	मोदो
320.	map	mapa	map	*maapa*	मापा
321.	March	marzo	March	*maar-so*	मारसो
322.	Mary	maría	Mary	*maariya*	मारिया
323.	May	mayo	May	*māayō*	मायो
324.	meal, dinner	comida	meal, dinner	*kōmiidāa*	कोमीदा
325.	meat	carne	meat	*kaaeney*	कारने
326.	meet, find	encontrar	meet, find	*n-cone-taar*	एन्कोन्त्रार
327.	memory	memoria	memory	*maymoriya*	मेमोरिया
328.	mention	mencionar	mention	*men-c-o-naar*	मेनसीयोनार

329.	mexican	mexicano	mexican	*maykhiikāano*	मेखिकानो
330.	mexico	México	mexico	*maykhiiko*	मेखिको
331.	middle, center	centro	middle, center	*sen-trô*	सेन्त्रो
332.	mile	milla	mile	*miiya*	मिल्या
333.	milk	leche	milk	*layche*	लेचे
334.	mine	mina	mine	*miināa*	मिना
335.	mineral	minaral	mineral	*miinayraal*	मिनेराल
336.	minute	minuto	minute	*miinootō*	मिनुतो
337.	Miss	señorita	Miss	*sen-yoritaa*	सेन्योरिता
338.	mistake	falta	mistake	*faal-tāa*	फाल्ता
339.	modern	moderno	modern	*mo-deyr-no*	मोदेरनो
340.	Monday	lunes	Monday	*loo-ness*	लूनेस
341.	money	dinero	money	*dii-nay-ro*	दिनेरो
342.	month	mes	month	*mace*	मेस
343.	more	más	more	*maas*	मास

344.	morning	mañana	morning	*manyaana*	मान्याना
345.	mother	madre	mother	*māadrey*	मादरे
346.	mountain	montaña	mountain	*mōntāanyā*	मोन्तान्या
347.	movies	cine	movies	*c-nay*	सीने
348.	Mr., Sir	señor	Mr., Sir	*sen-yor*	सेन्योर
349.	Mrs.	señora	Mrs.	*sen-yoraa*	सेन्योरा
350.	much	mucho	much	*moo-cho*	मुचो
351.	muchacha	muchacho	muchacha	*moochāacho*	मुचाचो
352.	museum	museo	musemuseou	*moosay-o*	मुसेओ
353.	music	música	music	*moosiikāa*	मुसिका
354.	my	mi	my	*mii*	मी
355.	my	mío	my	*mii-o*	मियो
356.	name	nombre	name	*nōm-brey*	नोम्ब्रे
357.	narrow	estrecho	narrow	*ace-trey-cho*	एस्त्रेचो
358.	natural	natural	natural	*naatūraal*	नातूराल

359.	near	cerca de	near	*sēerka dey*	सेरका दे
360.	necessary	necesario	necessary	*naysaysariyo*	नेसेसारियो
361.	necessary	preciso	necessary	*pray-c-so*	प्रेसिसो
362.	necktie	corbata	necktie	*kōr-baata*	कोरबाता
363.	need	necesitar	need	*naysaysiitāar*	नेसेसितार
364.	neither	ni	neither	*nii*	नी
365.	nevertheless	embargo	nevertheless	*M-bar-go*	एम्बारगो
366.	new	nuevo	new	*nooēevō*	नुयेवो
367.	newspaper	periódico	newspaper	*payriyodiko*	पेरियोदिको
368.	next	próximo	next	*proksimo*	प्रोक्सीमो
369.	night	noche	night	*nō-che*	नोचे
370.	nine	nueve	nine	*nooēevey*	नुयेवा
371.	ninety	noventa	ninety	*no-vēentāa*	नोवेन्ता
372.	no	ninguno	no	*niingoono*	नीनगूनो
373.	no	no	no	*no*	नो

374.	nobody	nadie	nobody	*nāadii-a*	नादिए
375.	North	América del Norte	North	*āamayrüka del nōrtēe*	आमेरिका देल नोरते
376.	north	norte	north	*nor-tēe*	नोरते
377.	notebook	cuaderno	notebook	*kooadēerno*	कुआदेरनो
378.	nothing	nada	nothing	*nāadā*	नादा
379.	novel	novela	novel	*no-vēe-lāa*	नोवेला
380.	november	noviembre	november	*no-v-m-brey*	नोविएम्ब्रे
381.	now	ahora	now	*āa-oraa*	आओरा
382.	occupied	ocupado	occupied	*okoopaado*	ओकूपादो
383.	October	octubre	October	*ok-tu-brey*	ओक्तूबेर
384.	of, from, than; in	de	of, from, than; in	*dey*	दे
385.	office	oficina	office	*o-fii-c-nāa*	ओफिसिना
386.	often	menudo	often	*maynoo-dō*	मेनुदो

387.	old	viejo	old	*vee-e-kho*	विएखो
388.	old,ancient	antiguo	old, ancient	*āantügao-o*	आन्तीगुओ
389.	olive	oliva	olive	*o-liva*	ओलिवा
390.	olive tree	olivo	olive tree	*o-lèvo*	ओलिवो
391.	on arriving	al llegar	on arriving	*āal Yegāar*	आल येगार
392.	on, upon	al	on, upon	*āal*	आल
393.	only	solo	only	*solo*	सोलो
394.	open	abrir	open	*āa-brür*	आबरीर
395.	opportunity	oportunidad	opportunity	*o-por-tuniidad*	ओपोरतूनिदाद
396.	opportunity	otoño	opportunity	*o-tōn-yo*	ओतोन्यो
397.	or	o	or	*o*	ओ
398.	orange	naranja	orange	*nāarankhaa*	नारान्खा
399.	orange tree	naranjo	orange tree	*nāarāankho*	नारान्खो
400.	ought, should, must	deber	ought, should, must	*dey-bēer*	देबेर

401.	our	nuestro	our	*nooestrō*	नुएस्त्रो
402.	overcoat	gabán	overcoat	*gaabaan*	गाबान
403.	page	página	page	*pāakhiinaa*	पारवीना
404.	painting	pintura	painting	*pintūrāa*	पिन्तूरा
405.	palace	palacio	palace	*pāalāa-c-o*	पालासियो
406.	paper	papel	paper	*paapale*	पापेल
407.	part	parte	part	*paar-tēe*	पारते
408.	pass, spend (time)	pasar	pass, spend (time)	*paasaar*	पासार
409.	Paul	Pablo	Paul	*paablo*	पाबलो
410.	pay	pagar	pay	*pāgāar*	पागार
411.	pen	pluma	pen	*ploo-maa*	प्लूमा
412.	pencil	lápiz	pencil	*lāapiz*	लापिस
413.	people, crowd	gente	people, crowd	*khentēe*	खेन्ते
414.	perfect	perfecto	perfect	*ppayrfekt*	पेरफेक्तो

415.	person	persona	person	*payr-so-na*	पेरसोना
416.	petroleum, oil	petróleo	petroleum, oil	*paytrolayo*	पेत्रोलेयो
417.	picture	cuadro	picture	*kooadro*	कुआद्रो
418.	picturesque	pintoresco	picturesque	*pin-to-resko*	पिन्तोरेस्को
419.	pity	lástima	pity	*lāastimāa*	लासतिमा
420.	place, put	poner	place, put	*pō-nay-er*	पोनेर
421.	plain	llanura	plain	*yaanoora*	ल्यानूरा
422.	play	jugar	play	*khoogāar*	खूगार
423.	please	gustar	please	*goosrāar*	गुस्तार
424.	poet	poeta	poet	*pō-a-tāa*	पोएता
425.	poetic	poético	poetic	*pō-a-tikō*	पोएतिका
426.	poor	pobre	poor	*pōbrey*	पोब्रे
427.	possible	posible	possible	*pō-c-bley*	पोसिब्ले
428.	post office	casa de correos	post office	*kaasa dey korey-os*	कासा दे कोर्रेओस

429.	potato	patata	potato	*paatata*	पाताता
430.	practice	práctica	practice	*prāaktiikāa*	प्राक्तिका
431.	prefer	preferir	prefer	*pray-fayreer*	प्रेफेरिर
432.	prepare	preparar	prepare	*praypaaraar*	प्रेपारार
433.	pretty	bonito	pretty	*bōneetō*	बोनितो
434.	principal	principal	principal	*preen-c-paal*	प्रिन्सीपाल
435.	probable	probable	probable	*probabley*	प्रोबाबले
436.	produce	producir	produce	*prodoociir*	प्रोदूसिर
437.	professor	profesor	professor	*profaysōr*	प्रोफेसोर
438.	progress	progreso	progress	*pro-grey-so*	प्रोग्रेसो
439.	pronounce	pronunciar	pronounce	*pronoonsiaar*	प्रोनुन्सीयार
440.	pronunciation	pronunciación	pronunciation	*pro-nun-c-acion*	प्रोनुन्सीयासीयोन
441.	public square	plaza	public square	*plāasāa*	प्लासा
442.	public-	edificio	public-	*A-dii-fii-C-O*	एदिफीसिओ

	building		building		
443.	publish	publicar	publish	*ppubliipaar*	पुब्लिकार
444.	pull out, draw out	sacar	pull out, draw out	*sāa-kar*	साकार
445.	pupil	alumno	pupil	*āaloomno*	आलुमनो
446.	queen	reina	queen	*ree-ina*	रेइना
447.	railroad	ferrocárril	railroad	*ferrōkāaril*	फेरोकारील
448.	rain	llover	rain	*yovēer*	ल्योवेर
449.	read	leer	read	*lay-ēer*	लेएर
450.	receive	recibir	receive	*re-ci-bir*	रेसिबिर
451.	red	rojo	red	*ro-kho*	रोखो
452.	relation	relación	relation	*re-laa-sion*	रेलासियोन
453.	relative	pariente	relative	*pāarii-n-tēe*	पारिएन्ते
454.	remain, stay	quedar	remain, stay	*ke-dáar*	केदार
455.	remember	recordar	remember	*re-ko-r-dar*	रेकोरदार

456.	repeat	repetir	repeat	*re-pii-tir*	रेपेतिर
457.	repetition	repetición	repetition	*repe-ti-sion*	रेपेतिसियोन
458.	rest	descansar	rest	*des-kaan-saar*	देसकान्सार
459.	restaurant	restaurante	restaurant	*res-tāa-ooraante*	रेस्ताउरान्ते
460.	return	volver	return	*vol-ver*	भोलभेर
461.	rever	nunca	rever	*noonkāa*	नुनका
462.	review	repasar	review	*re-pāasar*	रेपासार
463.	review	repaso	review	*re-paso*	रेपासो
464.	rich	rico	rich	*ree-ko*	रिको
465.	riches,wealth	riqueza	riches, wealth	*ree-ke-sāa*	रिकेसा
466.	right, reason	razón	right, reason	*rāa-son*	रासोन
467.	river	río	river	*ree-io*	रियो
468.	road	camino	road	*kāamüno*	कामिनो
469.	Robert	Roberto	Robert	*ro-berto*	रोबेरतो
470.	room	cuarto	room	*kooartō*	कुआर्तो

471.	rule	regla	rule	*re-glaa*	रेगला
472.	run	correr	run	*kō-rēer*	कोर्रे
473.	sad	triste	sad	*tri-ste*	त्रिस्ते
474.	same	mismo	same	*miismo*	मिसमो
475.	Saturday	sábado	Saturday	*sāa-baado*	साबादो
476.	say, tell	decir	say, tell	*dey-seer*	देसीर
477.	school	escuela	school	*s-koo-a-lāa*	एसे, एसा
478.	scold	regañar	scold	*re-gāa-nyar*	रेगान्यार
479.	second	segundo	second	*se-goondo*	सेगुन्दो
480.	see	ver	see	*ver*	वेर
481.	sell	vender	sell	*ven-der*	वेन्देर
482.	sentence	frase	sentence	*fraa-say*	फ्रासे
483.	September	septiembre	September	*sep—ti-embre*	सेप्तीएमबवे
484.	serve	servir	serve	*ser-vir*	सेरविर
485.	seven	siete	seven	*si-ete*	सिएते

486.	seventy	setenta	seventy	*se-tentaa*	सेतेन्ता
487.	shave	afeitar	shave	*āafēeitāar*	आफेइतार
488.	she, it	ella	she, it	*A-ya*	एल्या
489.	shirt	camisa	shirt	*kāamüsa*	कामिसा
490.	shoe	zapato	shoe	*saa-paa-to*	सापातो
491.	shopping	compra	shopping	*kōm-prāa*	कोम्प्रा
492.	shore store	zapatería	shore store	*sāa-pāa-teriaa*	सापातेरिया
493.	short	corto	short	*kōrtō*	कोर्तो
494.	show	mostrar	show	*mōstrāar*	मोसत्रार
495.	sick	enfermo	sick	*n-fer-mo*	एन्फेरमो
496.	sight, view	vista	sight, view	*ve-stāa*	विस्ता
497.	silk	seda	silk	*se-dāa*	सेदा
498.	silver	plata	silver	*plāata*	प्लाता
499.	similar	semejante	similar	*se-me-khante*	सेमेखान्ते
500.	simple	sencillo	simple	*sen-ci-lyo*	सेन्सियो

501.	sing	cantar	sing	*kāantaar*	कान्तार
502.	sit down	sentarse	sit down	*sen-tarse*	सेन्तारसे
503.	six	seis	six	*se-ees*	सेइस
504.	sixty	sesenta	sixty	*se-sentaa*	सेसेन्ता
505.	sleep	dormir	sleep	*dōr-miir*	दोरमीर
506.	sleep	sueño	sleep	*soo-e-nyo*	सूएन्यो
507.	slowly	lentamente	slowly	*lentāamentēe*	लेन्तामेन्ते
508.	small	pequeño	small	*pay-kenyo*	पेकेन्यो
509.	smoke	fumar	smoke	*foo-māar*	फुमार
510.	some, any	alguno	some, any	*āalgoono*	आलगुनो
511.	something else	cosa	something else	*kōsāa*	कोसा
512.	something, anything	algo	something, anything	*āalgo*	आलगो
513.	son(daughter)	hijo	son(daughter)	*iijo*	ईखो

514.	soon	pronto	soon	*prōn-tō*	प्रोन्तो
515.	soup	sopa	soup	*so-pāa*	सोपा
516.	South	América del Sur	South	*āamayrüka del soor*	आमेरिका देल सुर
517.	south	sur	south	*soor*	सूर
518.	Spain	España	Spain	*Ace-panya*	एस्पान्या
519.	Spanish	español	Spanish	*acepanyol*	एस्पान्योल
520.	speak	hablar	speak	*āablāar*	आबलार
521.	spring	primavera	spring	*preemavayraa*	प्रिमावेरा
522.	spring, source	fuente	spring, source	*foo-n-tēe*	फुएन्ते
523.	square	cuadrado	square	*kooadrāado*	कुआद्रादो
524.	stairway	escalera	stairway	*s-ka-lerāa*	एस्कालेरा
525.	station, season	estación	station, season	*acetāa-c-ōn*	एस्तासिओन
526.	still, yet	todavía	still, yet	*ta-dāa-viaa*	तोदाविया

527.	stocking	media	stocking	*maydiya*	मेदिया
528.	stop	dejar	stop	*deyphaar*	देखार
529.	store, shop	tienda	store, shop	*tee-e-ndaa*	तिएन्दा
530.	street	calle	street	*kayēe*	काय्ये
531.	student	estudiante	student	*acetū-diiyantēe*	एस्तुदिआन्ते
532.	study	estudiar	study	*acetū-diiyaar*	एस्तुदिआर
533.	subway	metro	subway	*maytro*	मेत्रो
534.	subway	subterráneo	subway	*soob-te-rrāaneo*	सूबतेरानेयो
535.	such, such a	tal	such, such a	*taal*	ताल
536.	sugar	azúcar	sugar	*asaokāar*	आसूकार
537.	suit of clothes	traje	suit of clothes	*traa-khe*	त्राखे
538.	summer	verano	summer	*ve-rāano*	वेरानो
539.	sun	sol	sun	*sol*	सोल
540.	Sunday	domingo	Sunday	*dō-miin-go*	दोमींगो
541.	surround	rodear	surround	*ro-dear*	रोदेयार

542.	swim	nadar	swim	*naadāar*	नादार
543.	table	mesa	table	*maysāa*	मेसा
544.	tailor	sastre	tailor	*sāa-stre*	सास्त्रे
545.	tailor shop	sastrería	tailor shop	*sāa-steria*	सास्त्रेरिया
546.	take	tomar	take	*to-māar*	तोमार
547.	take leave of, say good-bye to	despedirse de	take leave of, say good-bye to	*des-pay-diir-say-dey*	देस्पेदीरसे दे
548.	taste	gusto	taste	*goostō*	गूस्तो
549.	teach, show	enseñar	teach, show	*n-senyaar*	एन्सेन्यार
550.	teacher, master	maestro	teacher, master	*māaestro*	माएस्तेरो
551.	ten	diez	ten	*dii-s*	दिएस
552.	thank you	gracias	thank you	*graa-c- āas*	ग्रासीआस
553.	that (one), the	aquél,	that (one), the	*āakayl, āakayāa*	आकेल

	former	aquélla	former		
554.	that, those	ese, esa	that, those	*Λ-say, Λ-sāa*	एसे, एसा
555.	the rest, the others	demás	the rest, the others	*dey-maas*	देमास
556.	the United states	estado	the United states	*ace-tāar*	एस्तादो
557.	theater	teatro	theater	*ti-āa-tro*	तीआत्रो
558.	then	después	then	*de-poo-s*	देस्पुएस दे
559.	then	entonces	then	*n-tōn-cess*	एन्तोन्सेस
560.	then	luego	then	*loo-a-go*	लुएगो
561.	there	allí	there	*āaii*	आइ
562.	there is	hay	there is	*aaii*	आई
563.	they	ellos	they	*A-yōs*	एल्योस
564.	think	pensar	think	*pen-saar*	पेन्सार
565.	third	tercero	third	*tero-sero*	तेरसेरो

566.	thirst	sed	thirst	*se-d*	सेद
567.	thirteen	trece	thirteen	*tre-se*	त्रेसे
568.	thirty	treinta	thirty	*tre-i-ntáa*	त्रेईन्ता
569.	this, these	este, esta	this, these	*ace-tēe, ace-tāa*	एस्ते, एस्ता
570.	thousand	mil	thousand	*miil*	मिल
571.	three	tres	three	*tre-s*	त्रेस
572.	Thursday	jueves	Thursday	*khoo-a-vess*	खूवेएस
573.	thus, so	así	thus, so	*asee*	आसि
574.	time	vez	time	*ves*	वेस
575.	time, weather	tiempo	time, weather	*tee-e-mpo*	तिएम्पो
576.	tip	propina	tip	*propeena*	प्रोपीना
577.	tired	cansado	tired	*kāansāadō*	कान्सादो
578.	to, up to	hasta	to, up to	*aas-tāa*	आस्ता
579.	today	hoy	today	*oii*	ओई
580.	too, too much	demasiado	too, too much	*dey-maa-c- āado*	देमासियादो

581.	train	tren	train	*tre-n*	त्रेन
582.	tranquil, quiet	tranquilo	tranquil, quiet	*tráa-n-killa*	त्रान्किलो
583.	translate	traducir	translate	*tráa-doo-sir*	त्रादुसिर
584.	translation	traducción	translation	*tráa-doo-ksion*	त्रादुक्सियोन
585.	travel	viajar	travel	*vee-a-khāar*	वियाखार
586.	tree	árbol	tree	*āarbole*	आरबोल
587.	trip, journey	viaje	trip, journey	*vee-aa-khe*	वियाखे
588.	truth	verdad	truth	*ver-dāad*	वेरदाद
589.	try	tratar	try	*tráātáar*	त्रातार
590.	Tuesday	martes	Tuesday	*māartēss*	मारतेस
591.	twelve	doce	twelve	*dō-say*	दोसे
592.	twenty	veinte	twenty	*ve-inte*	वेइन्ते
593.	two	dos	two	*dōs*	दोस
594.	uncle	tío	uncle	*ti-o*	तियो
595.	understand	comprender	understand	*kōm-pren-dēer*	कोम्प्रेन्देर

596.	university	universidad	university	*.oo-nee-ver-see daad*	यूनिवेरसिदाद
597.	useful	útil	useful	*ooteel*	ऊतिल
598.	vacant, empty	vacío	vacant, empty	*vaa-sio*	भासियो
599.	vacation	vacaciones	vacation	*vaa-ka-sio-ness*	भाकासियोन
600.	vegetable	legumbre	vegetable	*laygoombrey*	लेगुम्बरे
601.	very	muy	very	*mooii*	मुई
602.	village	pueblo	village	*pooeblow*	पुएब्लो
603.	visit	visitar	visit	*vee-see-táar*	विसितार
604.	vocabulary	vocabulario	vocabulary	*voca-boo-laario*	बोकाबुलारियो
605.	waiter	mozo	waiter	*mōsō*	मोसो
606.	wake up	despertarse	wake up	*des-per-tāar-say*	देस्पेरतारसे
607.	walk	andar	walk	*āandāar*	आन्दार
608.	walk	paseo	walk	*paasay-o*	पासेओ
609.	wall	pared	wall	*paarēed*	पारेद

610.	wash	lavar	wash	*lāavāar*	लावार
611.	watch	reloj	watch	*re-lokh*	रेलोख
612.	water	agua	water	*āagooa*	आगुवा
613.	we	nosotros	we	*no-sō-trōs*	नोसोत्रोस
614.	Wednesday	miércoles	Wednesday	*mii-er-ko-less*	मिएरकोलेस
615.	week	semana	week	*se-maanaa*	सेमाना
616.	well	bien	well	*B-N*	बिएन
617.	what, which	¿qué?	what, which	k	के
618.	which, what	cuál	which, what	*kooal*	कुआल
619.	wheat	trigo	wheat	*tri-go*	त्रिगो
620.	when	cuando	when	*kooando*	कुआंदो
621.	where	donde	where	*dōn-dey*	दोन्दे
622.	while	mientras	while	*mii-n-trāas*	मिएन्त्रास
623.	white	blanco	white	*blāan-ko*	बलान्को
624.	who, whom	quien	who, whom	*ki-en*	किएन

625.	who, whom that which	que	who, whom, that which	k	के
626.	whose, of whom of which	cuyo	whose, of whom, of which	kooyo	कूयो
627.	why?	¿por qué?	why?	¿põr kay?	पोरके
628.	window	ventana	window	ven-taana	वेन्ताना
629.	wine	vino	wine	vee-no	विनो
630.	winter	invierno	winter	inve erno	इनवियेरनो
631.	wish, desire	desear	wish, desire	dey-say-r	देसेआर
632.	wish, love	querer	wish, love	ke-reer	केरेर
633.	with	con	with	cone	कोन
634.	with me	conmigo	with me	cone-mügo	कोनमीगो
635.	without	sin	without	sin	सिन
636.	woman	mujer	woman	moopher	मुखेर

637.	wool	lana	wool	lāa-nāa	लाना
638.	word	palabra	word	pāalāabrā	पालाब्रा
639.	work	obra	work	o-brāa	ओबरा
640.	work	trabajar	work	traa-baa-khāar	त्राबाखार
641.	work	trabajo	work	traa-ba-kho	त्राबाखो
642.	world	mundo	world	moondõ	मुन्दो
643.	worse	peor	worse	pay-or	पेओर
644.	worth	valer	worth	vaa-ler	भालेर
645.	write	escribir	write	s-krii-biir	एस्क्रीबीर
646.	writer	escritor	writer	s-krii-tõr	एस्कूचार
647.	year	año	year	āanyo	आन्यो
648.	yellow	amarillo	yellow	āamarüyo	आमारियो
649.	yes	sí	yes	see	सी
650.	yesterday	ayer	yesterday	āayéer	आइयेर
651.	you	tú	you	tóo	तू